Many Languages, One Classroom

by Karen N. Nemeth

Acknowledgments

Because language is practically nothing without the relationships that give it life:

In awe of my daughters, Leah and Larissa, who started out as my inspiration, then grew up to be wonderful teachers, and are now my valued advisors.

In memory of my mom, Joan "Ty" Nelson, who touched the lives of thousands of young children throughout her teaching career and inspired me to love their language.

In appreciation of Marc Bjorkman, whose persistent support and insightful collaboration helped me get this book off the ground.

In gratitude for Gryphon House editors Kathy Charner and Kate Kuhn, who graciously shared their expertise and helped me learn to look at my own words in a whole new way.

Thank you all!

Also by Karen Nemeth: Many Languages, Building Connections: Supporting Infants and Toddlers Who Are Dual Language Learners

Many Languages, One Classroom

Teaching Dual and English Language Learners

Karen N. Nemeth
Illustrated by Chris Wold Dyrud

Gryphon House
Lewisville, NC

© 2009 Karen Nemeth
Published by Gryphon House, Inc.
PO Box 10, Lewisville, NC 27023
800.638.0928 (toll free); 877.638.7576 (fax)

Visit us on the web at www.gryphonhouse.com

Cover Art: Straight Shots Product Photography, Ellicott City, MD © 2007.
Illustrations: Chris Wold Dyrud.

Reprinted December 2015

Library of Congress Cataloging-in-Publication Information
Nemeth, Karen.
 Many languages, one classroom / by Karen Nemeth.
    p. cm.
 ISBN 978-0-87659-087-4
 1. English language--Study and teaching (Preschool)--United
States--Foreign speakers. 2. Second language acquisition--United States. 3.
Education, Bilingual--United States. 4. Education, Preschool--United
States. I. Title.
 PE1128.A2N3736 2009
 428.2'4--dc22

                        2009007021

Bulk purchase
Gryphon House books are available for special premiums and sales promotions as well as for fund-raising use. Special editions or book excerpts also can be created to specification. For details, contact the Director of Marketing at Gryphon House.

Disclaimer
Gryphon House, Inc. and the author cannot be held responsible for damage, mishap, or injury incurred during the use of or because of activities in this book. Appropriate and reasonable caution and adult supervision of children involved in activities and corresponding to the age and capability of each child involved, is recommended at all times. Do not leave children unattended at any time. Observe safety and caution at all times.

Table of Contents

Foreword

This book fills a serious gap in our professional toolbox: How to design and implement curriculum for young children who are learning English as they continue to learn their home language. As this is our fastest growing and most academically vulnerable segment of the preschool population, *Many Languages, One Classroom* is a welcome and timely resource. It is written for teachers and administrators who are faced with the daily challenges of meeting the linguistic, social, cognitive, and physical needs of children who are often adjusting to a new country while they are learning a new language. The suggestions and practices described are concrete, highly practical, and accessible for preschool teachers, while the overall approaches are based on current, rigorous research. It is written in a down-to-earth style that preschool teachers will appreciate; however, the content accurately represents the complexity of the scientific knowledge.

As I conduct professional development sessions around the country, one of the most pressing needs expressed by teachers and administrators is, "How can I promote overall language and academic development for my students who do not understand English," and "How can I honor the child's home language while fostering English acquisition?" *Many Languages, One Classroom* goes a long way toward answering both questions. A basic premise of this book—that we need to accept the languages children bring with them into preschool classrooms as linguistic strengths—is reflected in Ms. Nemeth's decision to use the term *dual language learners* (DLL) rather than *English language learners.*

The term DLL reflects the value of knowing more than one language, not just the goal of rapidly learning English, possibly at the expense of the child's home language. The need to value and support each DLL child's home language while also fostering English acquisition is consistent with current research on how bilingual children learn through both languages.

The author states her philosophy of early education for young dual language learners, "...our goal is not to teach children English...our goal is to teach children...and to help their English develop along the way" (page 20). This approach requires that teachers have deep knowledge of each child's language abilities, strengths, and needs so that the cognitive and linguistic demands can be adjusted according to how each DLL responds. No magic formula applies to all young DLL children or to the variety of early childhood programs that currently exist.

Deciding on the most appropriate strategy will require consideration of many factors: The personnel and financial resources available, the community values, the individual languages and backgrounds of the DLL children in each classroom, as well as the abilities of the teachers. Luckily, the curriculum suggestions presented in *Many Languages, One Classroom* contain a range of options that can be tailored to the specific conditions of any early childhood classroom. In fact, the specific activities described reflect good early childhood practices for all children—with adaptations that improve their effectiveness for dual language learners.

The chapters are organized according to seven centers (dramatic play area, outdoor play area, library reading area, small toy/manipulative area, writing area, science, and block area) and two daily periods (meal time and welcome/circle time). Included in each chapter are suggestions for materials, activities, links to state standards, home learning extensions, technology tips, and reflection questions for teachers. In addition, the author's extensive Introduction presents 10 basic principles for teaching dual language learners (see pages 20–22). These principles are clearly informed by current research and form the foundation for making appropriate curriculum adaptations for dual language learners.

One of the strengths of *Many Languages, One Classroom* is the concrete, practical nature of the strategies. The materials, activities, links, and extensions contain excellent suggestions for all early childhood educators, but are especially important for those working with children who are learning English as a second language. For example, the suggestion to use visuals, photos, body language, gestures, and facial expressions to reinforce the messages in the dramatic play area will help all children better understand the intended communication, but may be a critical aspect of engaging DLL children in the classroom activities.

Because all states that have public funding for preschool also have state early learning standards, the Links to Standards section in each chapter helps practitioners better understand how each particular lesson/activity promotes progress toward important content standards. Suggestions about using a welcoming activity during circle time to promote math and science concepts underscore the integrated learning of preschoolers across multiple curriculum domains.

I enthusiastically agree with the author when she asserts that during the next decade we will see a greatly expanded research base on young dual language learners. My hope is that this book will contribute to the bridging of the research world with the reality of practitioners who need research-based curriculum guidance, and that early childhood educators will be motivated to continue to learn new strategies as our knowledge of "best practices" for dual language learners continues to grow.

—Linda M. Espinosa, Ph.D.
Former Professor of Early Childhood Education
University of Missouri-Columbia
Columbia, Missouri

Introduction

Teachers work in increasingly diverse classrooms. Ten years ago, the teacher who asked me for guidance about supporting English language learners (ELLs) was the exception. Now most teachers have at least one child in their classroom who speaks a different home language. Not only are teachers encountering more children who are new to English, but they are also faced with an increasing variety of different languages. As challenging as these changes may be, an early childhood teacher's goal remains the same: To welcome all children and give them the best possible start in education and in life.

Even the most experienced teachers can feel a bit unsure about how to meet the unique needs of children from different language backgrounds. Early childhood teacher preparation programs devote little time to the subject of supporting dual language learners, and teacher-preparation programs for English as a Second Language (ESL) and bilingual education have not addressed the needs of the preschool age group.

The field of ESL teaching has been around for many years—and many wonderful strategies have been developed and tested. Unfortunately, most of these strategies work for children in grades K–12 who have a solid foundation in the language development process. Techniques developed for elementary school students are rarely appropriate for three- and four-year-old children who are just beginning to learn what language is all about.

A wealth of support exists for preschool teachers regarding ways to encourage both early literacy and language development in English. Preschool ELL children need both areas of expertise to come together in a cohesive approach in order to learn English successfully. It is up to the individual teachers and the programs and administrators who support them to make this synthesis happen.

Research to address this situation is now gaining momentum. We do not have any comprehensive studies that clearly chart the right path for educators to take when teaching preschool ELLs (Freedson-Gonzalez, 2008). Each teacher and each educational leader must decide what will work for the children they have in the context of the curriculum they use and the standards that guide them.

Research does show that children need to continue learning in their home language even as they begin to transition to English (Espinosa, 2007). According to Jim

Cummins (2008), "The research is very clear about the importance of bilingual children's mother tongue for their overall personal educational development." English language learners who receive good home-language support in preschool do better on preschool and kindergarten language/literacy measures in both English and their home language than children from English-only classrooms (Freedson-Gonzalez, 2008). Experts also warn that, without strong support of their home languages, children can lose their ability to communicate in those languages within two to three years (Cummins, 2008).

Full immersion in English with no attention to the home language has not been shown to offer any advantages for preschool learning or later academic success (August & Shanahan, 2008).

All preschool children should be taught, nurtured, and encouraged along a path that will enable them to succeed in school and in life—eventually with full command of the English language. Full immersion in English with no attention to the home language has not been shown to offer any advantages for preschool learning or later academic success (August & Shanahan, 2008). As educators and educational leaders, we need to celebrate bilingualism. Children are growing and thriving as bilinguals all over the world, and we want American children to have the same advantages. We know what should happen, but we do not yet have a body of research that can serve as a how-to manual for designing programs that foster bilingualism. How, then, can we turn our shared wish into a sweeping national reality?

Making Sense of the Terminology

An important step in the process of understanding and supporting language acquisition is to clarify the terminology we use. We have traditional terms for the educational approaches we use to teach children from diverse language backgrounds: The English as a Second Language (ESL) approach and the bilingual education approach. These two approaches use different paths to achieve the same goal: To help students become academically proficient in English.

The Language Acquisition Approaches Teachers Use

ESL and bilingual education programs or services are often quite separate in elementary and secondary schools in the United States. Teachers may specialize in one approach or the other. Colleges provide separate courses of study for each approach. States confer different certificates or licenses for ESL and bilingual education teachers. In preschool, where teachers strive to offer integrated, developmentally appropriate learning experiences for all children, these approaches can be much more effective when they are blended together.

Many countries that do not have English as their primary language encourage or require students to become fluent in English as well as their home language. In these countries, the term Teaching English as a Foreign Language (TEFL) may be used to describe their educational approach. While there are certainly differences between teaching English to non-native speakers in an English-speaking country versus a non-English-speaking country, many of the strategies described in this book will be helpful for teachers in both situations.

The national association for teachers using the ESL approach is called TESOL (Teachers of English to Speakers of Other Languages). The ESL approach focuses on using specialized strategies to teach non-English speakers in English. It is generally used in schools that do not have bilingual teachers or in those that choose not to teach children in their home languages. The establishment of ESL programs rather than bilingual programs can be motivated by the availability of suitable teachers and resources or by political and philosophical concerns.

Bilingual educators have their own association called NABE (National Association for Bilingual Educators). Bilingual education refers to instruction that takes place in the home languages of the students while supporting their learning of English. The decision to offer bilingual education depends on many factors, including the availability of teachers and resources that match the languages needed in a particular program.

A particular type of bilingual education that is growing in popularity in the United States is called "Dual-Language Immersion." In this type of classroom, there are children whose main language is English and children whose main language is something else—most commonly Spanish. In English/Spanish Dual Language Immersion, all of the children learn part of the time in their own language and part of the time in their new language. The goal is to help all of the children become bilingual together.

Supporting Children's Language Acquisition

The term used to describe the children who are learning in their home language, be that English or another language, varies depending on the context. The federal government asks schools to report the numbers of children who are Limited English Proficient (LEP) based on certain assessments. Funding is then directed toward providing supports for children who need added services. The problem with this terminology is that it focuses on a deficit in English rather than celebrating the strength of growing up bilingual. It can also lead to the mistaken assumption that a child who superficially seems to speak adequately in English does not need further support or services in their home language.

Research does not support this kind of misstep (August & Shanahan, 2008). We know that bilingual children may have a slightly smaller vocabulary in each of their early languages, but when they are assessed in both or all of their languages, they often have a combined vocabulary that is larger than the vocabulary of their monolingual peers. Bilingual children who do not receive adequate continuing support in their home language are likely to lag behind their peers in later school performance (August & Shanahan, 2008).

The Term *English Language Learners* (ELLs)

At the writing of this book, the term LEP is still required by funding sources as an official designation, but the use of the term outside of that context has begun to

Bilingual children who do not receive adequate continuing support in their home language are likely to lag behind their peers in later school performance (August & Shanahan, 2008).

decline. Another term that is used to describe children who have a home language other than English is English Language Learner (ELL). Some also use SLL (second language learner) but this is not as common. ELL gained popularity quickly because it helped educators move away from the deficit model and describe more accurately that immigrant children in classrooms in the United States are learning English.

However, there are some difficulties with this term as well. One problem is that this term does not describe the thousands of children from English-speaking homes who are enrolled in dual-language immersion programs or monolingual non-English programs intended to help them grow up to be bilingual. The information and strategies in this book are just as effective when teaching English-speaking preschoolers in Mandarin as they are when teaching non-English-speaking children to become fluent in English.

Another shortcoming of the term English language learner is that it has come to have a directional meaning. It can give the impression that the goal is to help all children move toward English and away from their home language. Certainly, the research and expert opinions cited throughout this book make the case that bilingualism is a skill that is desirable for all children in our country. It is not good educational practice to deny, diminish, or disrespect any child's home language. While we do want American children to become fluent and successful in English, this does not mean we want them to lose their home language.

To be successful lifelong learners, all preschool children need high-quality supports for early language and literacy development in language-rich environments with engaging and engaged teachers.

An important question also comes up when considering how to label children in preschool when they come from homes where the language is other than English. Although it is most common to hear teachers refer to these children as English language learners, the experts emphasize, "*All* preschool children are English language learners!" The term English language learner does not adequately describe the differences between a young child who is acquiring English as his first and only language and the child who is learning English in addition to her home language. To be successful lifelong learners, all preschool children need high-quality supports for early language and literacy development in language-rich environments with engaging and engaged teachers.

The Term *Dual Language Learners* (DLLs)

Most recently, a shift has occurred in the words that are used to describe young children in American preschools who come from different language backgrounds. NAEYC (see the December 2008 and February/March 2009 issues of *Teaching Young Children* and the March/April 2009 issue of *Young Children* for examples) has begun to replace the use of English language learner (ELL) with dual language learner (DLL). In October 2008, the National Office of Head Start organized its first National Dual Language Institute in Washington, DC. Renowned authors and researchers presented the latest information to Head Start administrators, consultants, and teachers to guide Head Start programs to focus on supporting both the home language and the development of English in diverse populations, as captured by the term "dual language learners."

Experts seem to agree that the newer term, DLL, strengthens the message that we must support each child's home language while we also scaffold their learning of English. In this book, DLL is most applicable because the information and strategies provided will be valuable for any teacher who is helping young children learn any language other than the children's home language. "Dual language learners" is a phrase that describes children who are growing up with some degree of bilingualism. It does not indicate a particular approach to teaching them. Dual language immersion programs, which are described on the previous page, are a specific way of implementing bilingual education. Dual language learners is a broader term that describes children regardless of the nature of their preschool program. The use of this term does not in any way diminish the commitment to ensuring that all children enter the American school system with the supports they need to succeed academically in English.

Many readers may be accustomed to using the term ELL to refer to their bilingual students. This book uses the term dual language learner (DLL) to emphasize the effort among experts to change the way we think of young children who learn other languages. The children are the same—only the label has been changed.

As time goes on, new terminology may come and go. What is most important, regardless of the terminology used, is for all early childhood educators to continue their professional commitment to ongoing learning. We must keep in touch with expert opinion from respected sources. We must be critical readers of research so that we don't just accept each new finding at face value, and we must continue to communicate with each other to learn and grow as professionals.

The Dual Language Continuum

Borrowing from traditional K–12 teacher preparation, educational practice for DLLs is divided into two categories: Bilingual Education where children are placed in a classroom with a teacher who conducts most or all of the lessons in the non-English language, or English as a Second Language (ESL) education where a specially trained teacher adds to the bilingual child's day by providing in-class or pull-out activities to help the child learn English.

In preschool, it is more helpful to think of a continuum. All high-quality preschool classrooms feature creative, active, individualized techniques to help children develop language and literacy. All preschool children are learning language, even if they are only learning English. Services for linguistically diverse preschool children can best be described by where they fit along a continuum from fully bilingual with emphasis on the non-English language to fully English with few supports for the home language (see below).

"Dual language learners" is a phrase that describes children who are growing up with some degree of bilingualism. It does not indicate a particular approach to teaching them.

Preschool DLL Supports Continuum

Fully bilingual teacher, mostly teaches in home language	Moderately bilingual teacher, teaches half or less in home language	Extensive use of ESL strategies, some home-language support	Moderate to minimal use of ESL strategies, rare home-language support, more English	English-only immersion, no home-language support

Whether a preschool program elects to offer bilingual education, ESL supports, or even a dual language approach (where speakers of English and speakers of other languages are in the same classroom and both learn the language of the others), strategies that fit with developmentally appropriate practice are necessary for all of these classrooms.

Some preschool programs purposefully set their classrooms up at one point along this continuum. Others offer a range of options and observe children to determine which part of the continuum fits their needs. Another category—dual language programs—combines some elements from both ends of this continuum. The goal of this type of program is to help all children become bilingual.

For many programs, the position of their classrooms along this continuum is purely a result of the language skills of the teachers teaching in those programs. Everyone has to work with the personnel and financial resources that are available to them.

Just as every program is different, so is every child. Some bilingual children have highly educated parents. Some children are read to frequently at home. Some speak home languages that have little, if any, written form. Some children come from families where reading is not a priority. Some speak a non-English language, such as Spanish, that appears frequently in the community and has many supports already available. Some children may have been adopted from a foreign country into a family and neighborhood where no one speaks their first language and nothing looks like "home." To determine what works, we must look beyond any single factor and consider the picture as a whole.

The characteristics of the teachers in each classroom heavily influence a program's effectiveness. It is difficult to find bilingual teachers in most parts of the United States. In addition, being bilingual is just part of the equation; what about classrooms with children who speak three or more different languages? Because of the complex demands of providing a high-quality preschool education, learning how best to support dual language learners is not a concern for teachers alone. Teacher preparation programs, curriculum trainers, and professional development providers must determine how they can integrate DLL strategies into all of their work. Administrators play a critical role in ensuring success for each teacher and for each child in any educational program.

How to Use This Book

Getting Teachers and Parents Involved and in Sync

This book is designed to help teachers and administrators with strategies that are easy to use and open for creativity. They are designed to fit the major constructivist preschool curriculum models, to address state standards, and to satisfy benchmarks of quality programming such as the Early Childhood Environmental Rating Scale (Harms, Clifford & Cryer, 2004), the NAEYC accreditation requirements (NAEYC, 2007) and Developmentally Appropriate Practice Third Edition (NAEYC, 2008), and Head Start Bureau guidance (Plutro, 2005). We may not have all of the answers yet about how to meet the needs of dual language learners, but the children cannot wait until we do. Remember, our goal is to provide high-quality preschool education for all of our children.

Preschool teachers and administrators frequently ask me how to address the concerns of parents and family members. Many parents and family members believe the best way for their children to assimilate into American culture is to jump fully into English and leave their home languages behind. They feel that support for their home languages will somehow slow their children down or relegate them to second-class status.

This sort of "sink or swim" belief goes against what the research and expert opinion demonstrate. While we always want to respect families' views and wishes for their children, we can show that respect by giving them the best information available. We must have confidence in our role as educational experts. We have a responsibility to share our knowledge with families and to provide them with a greater understanding of what will be most beneficial for their children. Keep sending the message that providing support for the home language is the way to achieve academic success in English.

Use a variety of different methods to help parents and family members see the value in home-language support. Throughout the chapters of this book, there are many different strategies designed to involve parents and families in their children's language development. It is so important to get to know each family so you can understand the hopes, dreams, fears, and concerns they have for their child. Some people are naturally resistant to change. Some family members are more comfortable speaking their minds than others are. It will take time and patience to get to know children's families, but the results are certainly worth the effort.

Getting to Know Dual Language Learners

It may also take some time to get to know the new dual language learners in your classroom. Tabors (2008) describes a "silent period" when new bilingual children may stop talking for some time as they adjust to an environment that is not filled with the same language they hear at home. Children are using this time to listen.

Think about the way infants develop language. They have the luxury of "listening" for about a year before we expect them to start speaking our language. By the time they start speaking, they already know a lot about how language works. Preschool children who are thrust into a new language environment also need time to listen and observe and begin to make sense of the new linguistic input (Jalongo, 2008).

Preschool children who are thrust into a new language environment also need time to listen and observe and begin to make sense of the new linguistic input (Jalongo, 2008).

Although your goal will be to fill each child's day with as much learning as possible, remember to give your dual language learners (DLLs) a break now and then. They may need quiet time to get away from the constant pressure to learn and communicate in a new language. Watch for signs that these children need some time to practice or absorb what they have learned—or time to be quiet and listen. We also want them to feel comfortable engaging in that all-important self-talk, described by Vygotsky (Bodrova & Leong, 2007) as a vital component of developing self-regulation and processing. Keep working on developing a warm, nurturing relationship with the children as they work their way toward true bilingualism at their own pace.

This same supportive, encouraging approach applies when a child begins to use his new language. Avoid correcting his pronunciation or grammar. Just as a toddler learns his first language, you should encourage the communication in the message rather than pick apart its correctness. If a child says "Miss Karen, a fire truck just drived in our driveway!" should I say, "Oh no, honey, that is not correct, say 'a fire truck DROVE down our driveway," or should I grab the phone and run to the window to find out where the fire is?

In the beginning, it is most important to help DLL children feel good about their attempts to talk to you. You might want to repeat what the child says, building in a little correction ("Thanks for telling me the fire truck drove in!") so the child can begin to hear correct usage. However, your primary reaction should be enthusiastic understanding and acceptance.

When we talk about young children's language development, it is important to consider the social and emotional factors that influence the pace and direction of that development. Think about your own experiences learning a new language. How do you feel when pronouncing a difficult word in front of other people for the first time? Some of us feel mildly embarrassed—some are practically frozen with self-doubt. For adults, learning a new language is partly about learning words and grammar, and partly about overcoming fear and inhibition.

Now, think about all the additional adjustments three- and four-year-old children who speak a language other than English at home have to make when they come to preschool for the first time. New country, new language, new people, new schedule, new food, new rules—children face all of these things while they are away from their families for hours every day. This is one reason why supporting a child's home language is so important. Strengthening family ties is in the best interest of all children.

The Big Picture of Language Learning

As educators, we have to pay special attention to the whole picture for these children to fully support their language learning. It is not good for any preschool child to feel helpless or left out. Preschool teachers need to focus on giving DLLs the kinds of experiences that will make them understand that they are valued members of the class and competent individuals.

Look for ways that all children can be helpers, sources of information, and can join in with group activities. Be clear with children that you will not tolerate teasing or bullying in your classroom. Take the time to scaffold cross-linguistic communication skills for all of children—skills that will surely be useful to children growing up in our increasingly diverse nation and in the global economy. For example, research shows that when children learn to notice, practice, and enjoy rhyming words in their home language as part of phonemic awareness, they generally transfer this skill easily to their second language (August and Shanahan, 2008). As long as children learn the concept of rhyming in their more familiar language, you do not need to be concerned if children do not learn rhyming words in English until elementary school years.

Supporting the social and emotional development of young bilingual children is necessary to ensure successful language development in both their home languages and in English. Language development, self-esteem, confidence, and security go hand in hand.

You will not find a one-size-fits-all curriculum or cookie-cutter lesson plans in this book. Instead, you will find a toolkit filled with ideas that knowledgeable and skilled teachers can mold to fit their own expertise and approach as they nurture each child along his own developmental path.

As early childhood educators, our goal is to teach children and help their English develop along the way.

We know just how varied and interesting those paths can be from one child to the other. With added language differences, the variations can be even more challenging. A strategy that is too difficult for one child might be too easy for another. A technique that works well for one teacher might fall flat for the next teacher. And a lesson that is effective for a child today will not be effective next month because that child will have learned more and developed further. So your teaching must grow with each child—and the information in this book is meant to support that growth.

Try the most basic strategies for the children who need them, and differentiate instruction to gradually scaffold more advanced learning of their own language as well as their learning of English. Meet each child wherever he is in terms of vocabulary and ability. At first, significant supports may be necessary all the time. Then, as the child learns and develops, you will gradually reduce the extra supports and increase the demands you place on the child to keep him engaged and challenged as he grows and learns. Most importantly, the goal is not to teach children English. That's a fine goal for high school, but it works against what preschool children need. As early childhood educators, our goal is to teach children and help their English develop along the way.

The chapters of this book are organized according to the main interest areas or centers in most preschool classrooms. Within each interest area you will find suggestions for:

- Materials and supplies to support children's home-language development as well as transitions to English;
- Activity enhancements for large groups, small groups, and individualized learning;
- Sample activity plans;
- Links to the main themes in state preschool education standards;
- Parent and family connections ;
- Technology tips that help to differentiate instruction; and
- Topics for reflection.

This book is based on the latest information on best practices that can guide us in all areas of the preschool classroom, throughout the preschool day. In general, teachers should provide some degree of daily support for each child in his home language. At the same time, teachers will begin to scaffold the transition to English. Each strategy in this book links to one or more of these principles:

- **Extend learning by maintaining themes for days at a time.** When children begin to learn English, they struggle to make connections between objects/ concepts and the words we speak about them. If you are doing an activity around water and fish—the child may begin to understand some basics. If you come in the next day and start talking about magnets—nothing from that child's learning the day before will be of use, and he will be back at square one trying to learn the words and concepts you are teaching. Themes or projects contribute to the scaffolding of learning in the new language and encourage content learning even while the child is not sure of the new language.
- **Use key word lists for each theme.** Create and use these lists to learn relevant vocabulary in each child's language. Do not be intimidated—it is easier than you think. If your whole staff shares this goal, you will help each other. If you are embarrassed to try to pronounce new words, just remember how much more embarrassing it is for a little child who can hardly communicate at all and sees no evidence of his familiar language while he is away from his family. Add the children's languages to classroom labels, and color code them so English is always in one color, Spanish a different color, and Polish in a third color, and so on. If Spanish appears on your labels in green, put green stickers on the Spanish books in the library area and Spanish CDs in the music area. Also use the Key

Words lists to introduce important words in English that will help DLLs gain meaning from the classroom themes.

- **Repeat and emphasize important words in English.** Teaching children from different language backgrounds requires teachers to be intentional in their speech. DLL children learn best when they hear simple vocabulary and short sentences. Try to use the same terms consistently for important things you really want the children to learn. For example, you might identify certain phrases that the adults will use for safety purposes on the playground. You might agree to use "Slow down!" instead of "Stop running." As each child progresses, increase the complexity of the language you use on an individual basis.

- **Whenever possible, include visual aids as part of communication.** Create a daily schedule with photos. Use more props and pictures. Point directly to pictures or objects when referring to them. These are called graphic organizers. Keep in mind what would help you if you were in another country where no one spoke your language.

- **Use body language, gestures, facial expressions, and American Sign Language to augment your communication with DLL children.** The most important thing is to take time to look the child in the eye, to focus on your interaction with him, and to show that you really care about the interaction. Not only will this help the DLL child understand you, but it also models for the other English-speaking children how to communicate with more than spoken words when playing with their DLL friends.

- **Make adaptations all around the classroom.** Having a few dolls of different skin tones, or a pair of maracas on the shelf does not make a fully multilingual/multicultural classroom. There should be models of each child's home language and culture in each area of the classroom.

- **Conduct home language surveys.** In addition to conversations with parents and family members, these surveys will help you to be clear about each child's home language and culture. For example, a child from India does not speak "Indian." There are many different languages spoken in India, and it is important to know which language is familiar to that child. Two children may speak Spanish, but one may come from a farm in Mexico and one may come from the bustling city in Puerto Rico. Their experiences will be vastly different, and teaching them effectively depends on respecting those differences.

- **Narrate play and activities.** Be more verbal throughout the day. Use purposeful language to capture those teachable moments when the DLL child shows interest. Help children make friends across language barriers by interpreting and describing the action until they begin to understand each other.

- **Use authentic props and real items to connect with each child's prior learning and help him to develop that language to talk about those things.** For example, children can use forks, knives, and spoons in different sizes and colors for counting games. Children know what these utensils are and have home-language vocabulary to help them as they progress and begin learning more sophisticated concepts. Also, the children have their shared vocabulary with family members, which makes it possible to talk about this activity at home.

- **Use the talents of your bilingual staff, volunteers, family members, and children.** Adults who know a child's home language should engage in rich, interesting conversations with that child. It is a sign of a high-quality program when all bilingual staff members are using their language to foster learning rather than just using it for classroom management. Do not be afraid to engage the bilingual children in activities that support and enrich the language interactions in the classroom. Invite a few native speakers of the languages the children in your program speak to form a "translation committee" (see below).

Language Advisory Committee

Form an advisory committee of parents, staff members, and community representatives. Parents who have a voice in their child's education will be empowered, even if they are not confident in their own language ability. Support from members of the community will help bilingual parents feel that there are plenty of shoulders to share the responsibility of giving their child the best early childhood education. Here are some suggestions for Language Advisory Committee tasks.

- Form a translation subcommittee to evaluate materials that have been translated to make sure they are accurate and appropriate for the audience— whether they are for parents, families, children, or even the press.
- The translation subcommittee could also assist by translating simple documents like the family newsletter or brochures. Individuals who speak another language are not necessarily skilled translators, but a group can work together to produce effective translations when needed.
- Committee members can write to contacts in their home countries to obtain authentic, culturally appropriate books, music, props, and games.
- Translate key words in popular storybooks in the classroom and put the translations (along with phonetic spelling) on stickers inside the books so the English-speaking teacher can read them.
- Provide translated labels, daily schedules, and classroom rules for the various classroom areas.
- Collect recipes from the different cultures represented in each classroom to use for lesson plans—and perhaps even a fundraiser.
- Organize family members and other volunteers to teach games and songs, read stories, join in nature walks, go on field trips, or just visit the classroom to have home-language conversations with the children.
- Visit local businesses, restaurants, yard sales, and flea markets to find free or low-cost items to use as language prompts, learning materials, and props in your classroom.
- Serve as advocates, cheerleaders, and fundraisers for your program.
- Create a rich, enticing language environment. At any point in the day, some children may be using their home language and some may not—but at all times, language should be the center of attention.

Now, let's see how this all works together in each center of the classroom.

Welcome Time/Circle or Group Time

1

Think About...

The following ideas and questions can help you relate authentically to each child.

☀ Plan to attend an event that is conducted in an unfamiliar language, such as a class for deaf adults conducted entirely in sign language, or a religious service or cultural event in another language. How did it feel to be an outsider? Could someone have done something to make you feel more comfortable? These experiences will help you assess your own welcoming strategies at your program.

☀ Is it time to consider changing the way you conduct circle or group time? Arrange visits to other classrooms or other schools to see new ways of using the morning welcome time.

☀ Observe your own language. View it through the ears of a child who is just learning English. Be sure it is clear and direct.

Set the Tone

Welcoming is an important part of every preschool program because it sets the tone for the day, the program, and the year. It fosters security, acceptance, learning, fun, and harmony for preschool programs in diverse communities.

What should welcoming look like? First, welcoming is not only for children. It is also the first impression you make on children's parents and family members. What do families see:

- As they drive by?
- When they enter your property?
- As they come in the front door?

When signs or announcements celebrate the languages of the community, parents and family members will feel that this is a place where people respect them and will welcome their children.

The morning rush is often the most frantic, stressful part of a working parent's day.

- Is your building easy to enter?
- Is there a friendly and supportive greeting procedure? Or will there be additional stress for the parent or family member who does not speak English and may not understand what teachers are asking or what is happening that day for their child?

Getting parents or family members involved is critical to the success of preschool programs and leads to continued school success; thus, the start of the preschool day also must be a positive start to every parent's or family member's day.

Finally, all children should feel welcomed and accepted from their first day of school and each day thereafter. They should see their home languages represented, their parents or family members interacting happily with staff, and children and family members should be able to chatter easily about what happens during the preschool day.

Reinvent Circle or Group Time

Although it has been traditional for preschool programs to have some type of whole group gathering at the start of the day, many of the newer curriculum models are reducing or eliminating that time as they increase attention to small-group learning and differentiated instruction. Now that we are firmly settled into a new century, this might be a good time to rethink some of the purposes of circle time and adjust to meet the needs of our changing population.

Try thinking of circle or group time as a welcoming time rather than a whole-group learning time. It is a useful time to connect with each child, help children re-establish their connections with each other, find out what is on their minds that might be incorporated into the learning of the day, and introduce what the day has in store for them.

Learn the correct pronunciation of each child's name. Adjusting to preschool is hard enough, and it is harder still when everyone is speaking a strange language. Names are not always easy to pronounce, but they are important to the children so it is well worth the effort to learn how to say them correctly! In addition, ask children's families what their children prefer to be called at school.

The Classroom Environment

Consider the following ideas for making the classroom environment welcoming for all children:

- ☀ Post welcome signs outside the building in English and in other languages.
- ☀ Post welcome signs and information in English and other languages where parents and family members enter the building.
- ☀ Post some welcome pictures/simple signs at children's eye level to make the children feel welcome and demonstrate the cultural and linguistic diversity of your program.
- ☀ Even with increased needs for security measures, try to make the entry of your building look soft, bright, and pleasant.
- ☀ Make multilingual or photo directional signs so visitors can find their way around the building.
- ☀ Create song posters of some favorite welcome songs. Use with hook and loop patches, like Velcro© or pockets where you can put the main words to the song, and add props to help children remember the words. For example, a poster with props like a smiley mask, a pair of stuffed gloves for clapping hands, and a pair of little shoes for stamping feet would illustrate, "If You're Happy and You Know It."

- Think about phasing out using a traditional calendar during circle time. Preschool children do not fully understand calendars because this kind of number listing (not really counting a quantity) and day memorization cannot be generalized. Instead of calendar talk, use this time to introduce and reinforce themes or talk about things that are important to the children.

Language Enhancement Activities

Consider the following ideas for making classroom activities welcoming for all children:

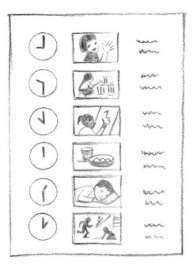

- Develop a welcome routine that helps DLL children get involved in an activity as soon as they come in and to ensure that they are not overlooked. Some teachers make sure that a small variety of calm and easy activities are set out when children arrive such as a limited selection of table toys, puzzles, small blocks, or books.
- When children arrive, make a special effort to greet each one warmly using their home language and an appropriate greeting. Ask the children's family members or ask your translation committee to help with this (see page 22).
- A daily schedule is an important part of a high-quality preschool program, and the comforting predictability of the schedule seems to be even more important for dual language learners. Be sure to inform children of any changes or variations in the schedule during welcome time. To help DLL children understand, refer to your photo schedule to show when any changes in the schedule will occur.
- Be clear about transitions. Use a universal warning signal, such as turning on and off the light, and a different signal when the time is up, such as singing a clean-up song or ringing a bell.
- Pass a ball around the circle and ask each child who gets it to say her own name and the name of the child who gets the ball next.
- Remember that telling and retelling stories is far more important to a child's literacy and language development than learning to sit still or wait their turn. We want children to work toward both of these objectives; therefore, during circle time try not to focus on one at the expense of the other. Use nonverbal cues to remind children about focusing and being respectful when their friends are talking. And make time for each child to say something important to you, a small group, or the whole group at least once or twice a week.
- Large-group gatherings should last no more than 20 minutes for preschool children.

Choo-Choo Train Tour

What You Need	Key Words
Train conductor hats Wooden train whistles Photo models that show how to use the materials and supplies in each area	All aboard! Follow me Go Station Stop Train Whistle The name of each interest center in your classroom

What to Do

- Before the children arrive, make sure that each learning/interest area in the classroom is set up with materials that will be the focus of learning in the coming weeks.
- Put on the conductor hat, or invite the children to be conductors.
- Blow the whistle and call "All aboard!" Ask the children to follow you around the room.
- Stop at each interest area and demonstrate how to use the space. Emphasize any key words or concepts in the children's home languages whenever possible, or in English supported by graphics and gestures to enhance understanding.
- Show the photo models to the children and remind them to check the models when they start playing in a center.
- After stopping at each interest area, take the train back to the circle area.

Extend the Learning

- Check for understanding. Whatever curriculum you are using, and no matter how many colorful, wonderful learning toys you have, children will not learn if they don't know what the toys are or how to play with them.
- Consider doing this Choo Choo Train activity every day for a week, and each day stop at a different center for a more detailed discussion and opportunity for children to ask questions.
- This Choo Choo Train activity could also be repeated for programs that conduct a review discussion with the children after they have had free play.

Links to Learning Standards

Math

* Use math in circle time activities to orient the children to the start of the school day and remind dual language learners (DLLs) to repeat vocabulary and names. Count and chart the number of boys present and absent, the number of girls present and absent, or the number of children that came to school in car, on a bus, or on foot.

* Replace the calendar ritual with other, more realistic daily starters that DLLs will understand more easily. For example, keep a chart of how many children use the word "warm" or "cold" to describe how the air felt on their way to school in the morning. Count the number of children present, and count the number of chairs at the tables to make sure they match.

* Use repetitive rhymes or songs for all children to enjoy together to incorporate the math concepts that you want to address, which will enhance DLL understanding.

Science

* If any of the children brought in natural items for the science area, identify the items and the role they play in the science area. Ask children to observe, compare, or share ideas for how to use the items. Have a language strategy in mind. If you want these discussions to take place all in one language, provide earlier or later opportunities for children who do not speak that language to repeat highlights of the discussion in their home languages.

* Welcoming time can be a good venue for "what if" questions that relate to current conditions or events.
    * It is pouring rain outside today. What if there were no umbrellas?
    * How would you feel if you wore a heavy coat on this sunny, hot day?
    * Now that it is fall, what would happen if we had a big tree right inside our classroom?

Think ahead and be prepared to use visuals to help children of varying language levels participate.

Social, Relationship, and Self-Regulation

* In a group of linguistically diverse children, some may be unsure or embarrassed about speaking in front of their peers. Do not make language an unpleasant experience for these children. Plan some aspects of the discussion so that several children could answer together. For example, have the children bring in a favorite stuffed animal. Invite several children to stand up together. They can show their beloved toys, even if they do not want to say a word. Ask questions that might have the same answer for each child so that all of the children can participate ("How does your animal feel? Soft? Furry? Scratchy?"). Then the children who have more to say can embellish without putting undue pressure on DLL children.

- Repetitive, predictable songs support the development of self-regulation and social skills during welcome time. Children who speak other languages can learn to stand still during the song until it is time to stamp their foot or clap their hands. These comforting and engaging routines also make it possible for shy children or new children to easily be an accepted part of the group.
- A circle time that is too long never works very well with preschool children. Consider using some of your ideas at other times of the day. For example, transitions can be great times for the children to practice a song or rhyme together. Perhaps you could have a bilingual conversation about the weather as the children are lining up to go outside.

Language Arts and Literacy

- Signing in (or attendance) can be an important part of the morning welcome. Early in the year, children can select their laminated picture stick from a basket and put it in a slot on the attendance board so all children can participate regardless of their language and writing ability. Include the child's name on his picture stick so that later he will be able to use this tool as a model for writing his name on a sign-in sheet.
- Some programs also post a "question of the day" to encourage children to practice their writing and letter recognition as they come in. By starting with simple questions represented by pictures, the concept of this activity can reach children of all language abilities. For example, there can be a picture of cereal and a picture of toast with space for children to make a mark under the item they want (or had) for breakfast. Next steps could include using more complex questions with home language words or by moving from pictures to part English rebus questions to all English questions.
- Use repetitive songs or rhymes as welcome songs that also emphasize language sounds and key words.
- When introducing the day's themes to a group of linguistically diverse children, use American Sign Language so that all of the children can share a common vocabulary of key words that will help them relate to the theme throughout the day.

Visual and Performing Arts

- Make beautiful bilingual signs. Add artistic styles that represent the cultures of your community. This could be a wonderful project to involve children's family members or volunteers from the community.
- Encourage children to talk with their family members about the artwork in your welcome area.
- Remember that music is an art form. Select authentic, beautiful music from different cultures and time periods, and help children play along with authentic ethnic instruments.

Family Connections

- Parents and family members do want information about the school day policies and procedures, but they may be too rushed to take in that information during drop-off or pickup times. Hand out information packets written in families' home languages to help them feel more connected with the program. For example, create a photo schedule of the day's events with pictures of clocks showing the time of day when each part of the schedule happens.
- Create a committee of parents and family members, staff, and members of the community to serve as an advisory council for your program. This group can provide so much valuable support to your preschool program and can be crucial in helping to meet the needs of a linguistically diverse student population. Establish a Welcoming Subcommittee to make sure there are materials and personal interactions to make each family or staff member feel welcome.
- If your school has a translation subcommittee (see page 22), it can check the information documents you prepare for families to make sure the translations are appropriate in meaning and complexity.

Classroom Technology Tips

- Make digital photos of children at their happiest during the day. Print out a couple of photos to hand to children's family members when they drop off their children in the morning to remind them that their children are happy, well-loved learners during the day.
- Use the recording capacity of your computer to capture the welcome songs you sing with your children. Burn the music onto disks to send home so families can learn and practice the language-rich songs at home with their children.
- Use a music-organizing program such as iTunes to create a playlist of songs you want to use at welcoming time. Once this list is loaded onto one or more mp3 players, teachers and children can easily access the favorite songs of the day to play them again in the music area, or to repeat a song during a transition time.

Questions for Teacher Reflection

Meeting the needs of dual language learners in preschool depends not only on your understanding of how first and second languages develop, but also on your cultural awareness. True cultural awareness requires significant self-awareness.

- Have you attended an event that was in an unfamiliar language? How can this experience help you assess your own welcoming strategies at your program?
- Are you considering changing the way you do circle time? Why or why not?
- Are you making conscious changes in your use of slang and replacing it with language that is clear for all children?
- How much do you know about the cultural background of each child in your class? What online, print, or community resources might help you learn more?

Dramatic Play Area

2

Think About...

* Talk to your colleagues about dual language learners' (DLL) actions during dramatic play and ask for suggestions to enhance the child's play, extend the learning, and support language development.

* When you notice the children are interested in a particular topic in dramatic play, what can you include in your lesson plan to take that interest to the next level for all children, including special supports for the DLLs?

* How do you know what the children are learning while in the dramatic play area? How can they show you if they don't speak much English?

* Read, "Young dual language learners, resourceful in the classroom" by Celia Genishi, (*Young Children*, July 2002). Share the article with your colleagues and discuss how to use the ideas to enhance your dramatic play area.

The dramatic play area of any preschool classroom can be fertile ground for learning. There is so much for children to talk about. When the teacher gets involved in play, it helps to broaden and deepen the learning significantly. This is the place where children rehearse all the different roles they see and care about. When the dramatic play area is full of developmentally appropriate materials, it can be the foundation for some of the most sophisticated and imaginative pretend play and language we see in preschool. It provides many wonderful opportunities for children to learn and to demonstrate what they are learning.

However, for children who do not speak or understand English, this area of the classroom can be much less useful. It is difficult to engage in pretend play with a group of children who are speaking a language that one child doesn't understand. It is difficult to gain much from a teacher who is sitting in the area and talking about things in words that the child does not comprehend. The child may attempt to communicate interesting stories using important vocabulary in his home language, but the teacher will not understand or be able to document any of those signs of learning.

Helping children communicate across the language gap is critical to facilitate the mature play that is so important to child development because it incorporates complex themes and scenarios, plenty of symbolic representation, well-developed roles for the participants, and the ability to maintain the play over time—even across several days (Bodrova and Leong 2007). Teachers and administrators must work together to ensure that all children receive a high-quality preschool experience in all its complexity. Too much focus on teaching preschoolers to speak and understand English will take away from the time they need to explore and understand their world and their roles in it.

Meeting Children's Language Learning Needs

All preschool children need three things: "exposure to varied vocabulary…, opportunities to be part of conversations that use extended discourse…, and home and classroom environments that are cognitively and linguistically stimulating…" (Dickinson and Tabors, 2003). Think about options in the dramatic play area and the resources available to you. How can you meet these needs for each child?

If you have bilingual staff, they can make these elements of language a regular part of their home-language interactions with beginning bilingual children. If you do not have adults on staff who speak the language of a particular child, try to find someone in the school or the community at large to help.

Even as you try to find bilingual staff or volunteers, you must continue to meet these three needs for your DLLs. Do not be afraid to use the English language with them. If you do not have full support in their home language, use as much of their home language as you can and supplement with all of your creative teaching talents to help them gain important language/content background in English. Yes, it will help to use simple vocabulary and sentences at first, but that doesn't mean you should never talk about a "glamorous" hat or a "delicious" pretend meal in the dramatic play area. Just try to be more intentional in your efforts to occasionally introduce interesting words.

Cultural Authenticity in Everyday Play

With some simple additions to the dramatic play environment and some new strategies for supporting play and learning in that area, you can help children from different language backgrounds become active participants in this important part of the preschool day. Take a moment to look at the dramatic play area. Do you see costumes and props that represent the cultural backgrounds of the children in your classroom? Begin by making sure the area truly represents the cultures of your children. Here is where the home language survey can be a big help. Not only will this make all children feel at home, but it will also show families of diverse backgrounds that they are welcome and respected.

Seeing this connection between home and school encourages parents and family members to have more conversations with their child about what happens at school instead of feeling that the school environment is a separate and foreign part of their child's experience. When the dramatic play area is full of authentic props, young children will find it easier to identify and talk about these items. The more connected the props are to the children's real lives, the more the children can use them to rehearse the roles they see in real life. Below are some ideas that can really bring the dramatic play area to life for your children within the context of implementing your chosen curriculum.

The Classroom Environment

Consider the following ideas for making the classroom environment welcoming for all children:

- ☀ Collect authentic clothing and accessories from different countries and cultures; ensure that the items are not "costume" pieces.
- ☀ Provide empty food containers from different ethnic food stores in the area.
- ☀ Look for utensils and appliances that children might see at home, such as chopsticks or tortilla makers.

- Offer maps, menus, newspapers, catalogs, and brochures in the languages of the children. Ask parents and family members to bring these items to school or reach out to your public library, local merchants, and restaurants.
- Label some of the items in the dramatic play area in different languages to help the adults use each child's home language when referring to these items during play.
- Offer books in different languages that relate to the common play themes.
- Bring some of these enhanced dramatic play items to the outdoor play area. If the DLL child begins to understand some of the English terms being used in the dramatic play area, he can expand on those connections if he sees the same items when he goes outside to play.
- Rotate props in the dramatic play area to keep interests fresh and/or to address themes in the curriculum. Make sure when you change the props in the dramatic play area that you also make similar changes throughout the classroom.

Language Enhancement Activities

Consider the following activities to support all children's language development:

- Add visuals to every aspect of the dramatic play activity. If you bring menus, make sure they contain photos of the food. Hang photos of people cooking over the stove, or place pictures of milk, eggs, and butter inside the refrigerator. Remind children and teachers to point to the pictures to augment their attempts to communicate with DLL children.
- When you enter the dramatic play area, remember to use more obvious body language, gestures, and facial expressions. This is an important area to support extended discussion for all of the children and must not be neglected for children who don't speak English.
- Think ahead about the themes that will be used in the dramatic play area. You might use one of the curriculum models that suggest themes, or you may just capture what children are interested in at the time. Provide the supplies that support learning in a particular theme without dictating how children should learn. Setting up some focused materials keeps the theme going and scaffolds learning over time for DLL children.
- Narrate the children's play to help the DLL children learn the phrases that fit in that context. In the dramatic play area, children are often acting out stories, which is a perfect opportunity for the teacher to inject rich vocabulary.

International Restaurant

What You Need	Key Words	
Restaurant menus that are familiar to the children (ask children's families to collect some)	bowl	stir
	breakfast	thank you
	chopsticks	warm
Magazines, catalogs, and flyers with photos of relevant food	cold	you're welcome
	cook	names of foods
Labels with food words translated into the languages of the classroom	delicious	appropriate to the
	dinner	props, languages,
	eat	and experiences of
Restaurant order pads	good	the children
Pens, pencils, markers, glue sticks, cardboard, or construction paper	hot	
	lunch	
Picture books about food, cooking, and restaurants	more	
	please	
Cooking utensils that represent the cultures in your classroom	restaurant	

What to Do

* Learn the key words in the languages of your classroom.
* Join the children in the dramatic play area to talk about the menus. Ask which is their favorite, do they remember the last time they were there, and what did they eat? Discover the foods they like, noticing words or letters they recognize, and so on.
* Participate in pretend scenarios about ordering at a restaurant, and preparing and serving food.
* Use food photos and paper supplies for children to create their own menus (discuss their choices with them and build on vocabulary and speech sounds as they come up).

Extend the Learning

* Plan a field trip to a local restaurant and arrange a tour of how things are made, served, and paid for. Take digital photos.
* Back at school, print out the photos and use shared writing and dictation to create a class book about the experience. Next, if possible, translate it into all the languages spoken in the class. Place the class book in the library area and bring some of the related books out of the library area to other areas where they could enhance play, such as the block area or writing area.
* Design food-related science projects or math activities for the small-toy area.
* At snack time, talk about the children's experiences of dining at restaurants with their family or friends.

Links to Learning Standards

Math

- Link dramatic play to math by having multiples of culturally relevant items. If you bring in chopsticks for dramatic play, have several of them in the small toy area for counting and sorting. Using connections from within the classroom or from home helps DLL children build on prior knowledge to learn new concepts. If they are already familiar with the items they are counting, they can devote their attention to counting rather than getting distracted by learning new vocabulary for the items they are using.

- Use math-oriented items in the dramatic play area that provide strong visual cues about math concepts, including clearly marked measuring cups and spoons, plates in different sizes or colors for sorting, play money, measuring tape to measure costumes or build things. Visual cues provide added information to help DLLs check their learning.

- Act out the concept of sequencing. This can make a big impact that cuts across language barriers. Use humor, for example, by dressing the baby doll and then putting it in the bathtub, or putting the pretend food on the table first and then putting the plate on top. Doing things in the wrong sequence encourages children to think and talk about how to make the right sequence. Scaffold to more sophisticated sequence demonstrations, such as acting out the steps to mailing a letter or the steps to get ready for a picnic.

Science

- Offer nonfiction books in different languages that relate to the play themes, such as books on different foods, on farming, on how babies grow, and so on.

- Post photos showing how things happen in sequence so children can begin to make guesses and predictions: ingredients, then batter, then cake pans going into the oven, then the finished cake coming out of the oven.

- Support dramatic play themes that involve investigation so DLL children (and all children) can actively practice science learning while role playing. For example, if you are working on a theme related to pets, have props and costumes about being a veterinarian; if you are doing a theme about the weather, provide small umbrellas, cloth jackets, and plastic rain gear.

Social, Relationship, and Self-Regulation

- Inviting DLL children to play may help if they seem shy. Adults can narrate play to help the DLL children make connections between words they are learning and the play activities in which they are participating. It helps DLL children feel more connected to the group and supplements their participation when they cannot express themselves clearly.

- Promote security and self-esteem by making props available that each child can relate to from their culture, their home country, or their local neighborhood: for example, Scandinavian ski clothes, dress-up shoes from China, fishing gear for children from coastal countries, or sari silks from India.

Just as we want all children to see themselves reflected in the books in the classroom, they should see their lives reflected in the role-playing opportunities of the dramatic play area.

☀ Learn key words in each child's home language. Teach those words to all the children. Showing respect for the child's home language has been shown to reduce the child's experience of isolation and helps the DLL child to be more accepted by the other children in the class. In describing their research on English literacy development, Dickinson and Tabors (2003) state that their "data strongly indicate that it is the nature of the teacher-child relationship and the kinds of conversations that they have that makes the biggest difference to early language and literacy development."

Language Arts and Literacy

☀ Use labels to encourage vocabulary development in all languages.

☀ Setting up themes can still allow children to have choices, but the overall theme sets up continuity of language acquisition that children can make sense of throughout the class through repetition.

☀ Make supplies available to practice writing in any language, including order pads, recipe cards, science notes, appointment books, and file folders.

☀ Offer relevant books in different languages.

☀ Extend conversations with children by referencing things outside the area. For example, when some children are pretending to go on an airplane trip, you might mention that one of them just got back from a trip to their home country and talk about the airport and the airplane experience. Ideally, this should happen in the child's home language, but attempt it in English if that is not possible. This is an important preparation for understanding books in later grades (Dickinson and Tabors, 2003).

Visual and Performing Arts

☀ Teach and encourage dance as a means of dramatic expression for anyone, regardless of their language ability.

☀ Allow children to create their own costumes for this area by painting T-shirts or coloring paper grocery bags. This self-expression is another avenue for communication for DLL children.

☀ The dramatic play area lends itself to actual drama by acting out sophisticated roles that communicate across language barriers. Go beyond pretend play to putting on the children's own fully developed short plays.

Family Connections

☀ Ask parents and family members to equip the dramatic play area with authentic items from their homes, their neighborhoods, or their countries of origin.

☀ Send home newsletters in each home language about the importance of pretend play. Encourage family members to ask their children about the dramatic play area.

- Take a picture of a child having fun in the dramatic play area and give it to his parent or family member at the end of the day. Imagine what it would be like if you had to drop your child off at school every day, but you did not have the language to ask the teacher how your child was doing? One photo of the happy child engaging in some interesting play would certainly go a long way toward helping parents and family members feel comfortable about their child's experiences.
- Ask family members to teach lullabies in their home language, and then encourage the children to use those lullabies when playing with the "babies" in the dramatic play area. If possible, record the songs and make them available in the music center.
- Call upon your Language Advisory Committee (see page 22) to help you stock your dramatic play area. Ask individuals to think back on their own pretend play experiences as children and see what creative suggestions they come up with for your program. They might be able to bring in donations or find useful props at yard sales or flea markets.

Classroom Technology Tips

- Use the digital camera to visually label what is in the dramatic play area. Create posters and class-made books about the activities that happen there.
- Take brief video clips of sophisticated play events to include in portfolios for performance-based assessments.
- Download linguistically appropriate materials from the Internet, such as menus from ethnic restaurants, word translations for labels, or pictures to use for dramatic play.
- Use podcasts to learn key words in the different languages to use during dramatic play.

Questions for Teacher Reflection

- How has your focus on the dramatic play area helped you to improve your planning for other classroom areas?
- If another teacher asked to observe your multilingual class, what are some of your most effective strategies that you would like to show him?
- What is one area of challenge for you that would be a good focus area if you observed another teacher?
- How did some of the DLL children show you what they were learning in the dramatic play area? How did they communicate with you?
- Did using a revised lesson planning form with specific strategies help you teach DLL children more effectively?

Outdoor Play Area

3

Think About...

Whether your program uses informal discussion groups or more structured communities of learning, questions that evoke memories of childhood experiences often lead to rich and valuable discussion.

☀ Think about your own childhood. What are your strongest memories of playing outdoors? Because you are an educator, reflect on what you were learning during that time. How can you duplicate those kinds of learning experiences for the children in your class now? How can you differentiate that learning for the language needs of each child? How can you document that differentiation?

☀ What are some of your favorite storybooks about the outdoors that you have in your classroom now? How can you find them or recreate them in different languages so all of the children can enjoy them?

☀ What does your current curriculum offer as guidance for making use of outdoor time? Does it provide specific guidance that will help you support dual language learners (DLL)? If not, what adaptations can be made?

Language plays many important roles in the learning that occurs outdoors, especially in ensuring the safety of the children. Even the safest playground can have its share of hazards as children are running, climbing, and exploring their environment. Any teacher who has ever supervised a playground knows how challenging it is to make sure everyone plays safely and harmoniously.

Imagine what it's like when you have a cold and cannot use your voice. If you have not had that experience, try to say absolutely nothing for 10 minutes while out on the playground with the children. You will begin to realize how often you depend on language outdoors—how many times you call out children's names, remind them of a safety rule, or talk some children through conflict resolution. You will notice all of the moments when you wish you could communicate with the children.

This lack of verbal input is similar to the experiences of DLL children in the outdoor environment. If the children do not understand the language that you speak, you have no way of knowing what safety rules they understand, what their skills are, or how they are processing all of the learning experiences available to them. Increasing your awareness of the need for language during outdoor experiences will enable you to plan more effectively to meet the needs of the children. This chapter is full of suggestions to get you started. Teachers, assistants, and volunteers can all help by learning needed terms in the languages of the children and by developing a repertoire of non-verbal communication techniques to make outdoor time safe, fun, and interesting for everyone.

Something to Talk About

In addition to the language connection with the physical aspects of outdoor play, think of all of the opportunities for conversation, vocabulary building, oral language, problem solving, and discovery that occur outside. The outdoor environment offers opportunities for the physical representation of the language that is being spoken, which can enhance vocabulary connections for DLL children. But teachers must address those connections intentionally.

This chapter presents ways to make the outdoor environment more meaningful to the DLL children in your care, and proposes a few activities to enhance the learning that occurs outside. These suggestions are meant to spark your creativity and inspire you to create your own outdoor activities.

The Outdoor Environment

Consider the following ideas for making the classroom environment welcoming for all children:

- Add authentic items to the outdoor area so DLL children will recognize them and use their home language to help them learn about their functions. For example, offer real gardening implements or realistic looking stop/yield signs in the riding area.

- Create a basic safety vocabulary guide in all appropriate languages to post outside for teachers to check for pronunciation when communicating with a DLL child.

- Based on the children's interests, bring dramatic play props outdoors that will enhance the context for the learning that happens naturally in outdoor play areas.

- Find culturally relevant outdoor toys. Children from Italy, Haiti, or South America might expect to see soccer balls on the playground. Children from African countries may be more accustomed to playing with rolling hoops, or games like hopscotch and jump rope. Children from Europe and Japan may be more likely to have experience with climbing equipment and swings.

- Once you see what captures the interest of the children outdoors, bring related conversation starters into various areas of the classroom. This extends and confirms the learning that begins outside. If children are tending a garden outside, have linguistically appropriate books about farms and plants in the library area. If they are fascinated by the ants they see in the playground, set up an ant farm inside and make bilingual labels and word models (cards or posters with words in English and the children's home languages that they can copy as they learn to write their notes) for observation logs in the science area.

Language Enhancement Activities

Consider the following ideas for making classroom activities welcoming for all children:

- Bring themes and studies out of doors. Props and toys can extend the learning that focuses on the favorite book of the week or the long-term project the children are working on.

- The playground is a great place to enjoy some repetitive music and movement activities. Use them to rehearse playground rules or to reinforce connections of home language concepts to new English words.

- Use clear and simple language repeatedly with DLL children to label the things they are playing with or their actions. It is easier to demonstrate important concepts like "up" or "down" or "slow" or "fast" when children are playing outdoors.

- Use body language to demonstrate the skills you want the DLL children to learn, such as throwing, catching, climbing, running, and jumping.
- Ask parents and family members to teach the children familiar terms for outdoor games, toys, and activities.
- Outdoor time is great for cutting loose and running free—but there is even more to be gained from the teachable moments that abound. You may magnify the benefits of outdoor time by encouraging the children to engage in more mature play. Teachers should support sophisticated pretend scenarios, real sustainable games, and complex exploration. This is how children from all language backgrounds build their understanding of concepts. These opportunities must be available for DLL children.

Our Big Board Game

What You Need	Key Words	
Plastic tablecloth, old shower curtain, or a Twister game sheet	Blue	Start
	Finish	Stop
Permanent markers	First	Three
A large cube—either a box or a purchased "picture cube" with clear vinyl sleeves	Five	Two
	Four	Wait
	Go	Yellow
Photos, words, and numbers to post on the 6 sides of the cube to become dice	Green	The names of
	Move	pictures you place
	Next	on the sides of
Labels for the spaces on the game board in the languages of the classroom—words that match what is on the sides of the cube	One	the dice
	Red	
	Roll	
	Six	
Costume items that allow the children to become game pieces, such as different hats, vests made of painted grocery bags, scarves, and so on		

What to Do

❋ Before the activity, set out the tablecloth or shower curtain, and use markers to draw a path along it of several squares the children will move themselves along during the game.

❋ Label the sides of the dice with pictures and the number or color words in all needed languages.

❋ Find one or two children who already know how to roll the dice and move along in a board game. Ask them to demonstrate.

❋ Begin the game with a few interested children. Review the words on the dice, have them roll, say the word that comes up on the die, and move forward one step for each syllable in the word the child said.

❋ Repeat the steps with the children, encouraging them to take turns moving along the board.

❋ When everyone gets to the end, everyone wins!

Extend the Learning

❋ Bring the same vocabulary indoors with labels and activities.

❋ Create a smaller, indoor version of the game board for indoor practice.

❋ Display various game boards in the art area to serve as models if children are interested in creating their own.

Links to Learning Standards

Math

- Consider bringing counting games outdoors in a much larger form. Bring large blocks and stacking and nesting toys to the playground to do counting and comparing activities. This gives you additional opportunities to demonstrate those critical math components in a way that is easier for children who are learning English.

- Take advantage of naturally occurring opportunities to emphasize counting words in English, such as counting the number of times a child gets the ball through the hoop or counting how many times they can hop on one foot, or how many pavement blocks are outside. Practice one-to-one correspondence by lining up the children and the bikes to see if there is a bike for each child. Making math connections with real-life events can help DLL children understand the math vocabulary and concepts.

- Measuring, recognizing patterns, and comparing can take on a grander and more realistic scale outdoors. Help DLL children gain a deeper understanding of math concepts by pointing out leaf patterns, tree rings, the number of windows on the building, or how many steps it takes to get across the playground.

- Count, compare, and estimate with easy-to-understand visual demonstrations. For example, when the children are lined up to go inside, announce that each child must carry three things back in the classroom. For the first child, count out three leaves. For the next child, count out three twigs. For the next child, count out three tennis balls. Then, for the next child count out...uh-oh!...three large playground balls! The demonstration gets even funnier when the next child is asked to carry three tricycles or three chairs.

Science

- Give children small bags to collect a variety of leaves. Spend some small-group time looking at the leaves and sorting them based on different characteristics. Some may sort by color, by texture, by size, or by the numbers of points on the leaves. In any of these cases, think about how much learning may be lost on a child who doesn't understand the language. Be more intentional in your use of gestures, repetition, and visual displays to help the DLL children understand. In addition, generalize concepts in other activities. For example, if some children sorted the leaves by color, help them read a book about sorting other objects by color, or chart shirt colors to continue the use of the oral language that supports this science concept. Providing the children with the vocabulary they need to participate in these discussions also provides them with nuances of understanding that make them better scientific observers.

- Capitalize on the interests you observe in the DLL children to help them frame questions that can be tested when you go outside. By doing so, you can help to build their vocabulary and their knowledge levels. When you introduce a teacher-directed, large-group science activity, you will not know which child has which prior knowledge of the topic, especially if your language does not match the child's. Do they like stamping shapes into playdough inside? Then you might set up an exploration of how footprints can be "stamped" in various surfaces outdoors. What happens if the children sprinkle a little water on the dirt, simulating rain? Is it easier or harder to leave a footprint? Do animals leave footprints?

Social, Relationship, and Self-Regulation

- Develop and practice nonverbal signals for learning self-regulation and transitions. Sing the same melody every day when it is time to go outside. Ring a bell to go inside. Use the American Sign Language signs for "stop," "all finished," and "more."
- Narrate the play of DLL children outdoors to help them integrate more fully into the play of their peers and help them learn the vocabulary that describes what they are doing.

Language Arts and Literacy

- Traditional chants and rhymes for outdoor games provide great practice for phonemic awareness in English and the home language.
- Use the many familiar signs in the outdoor environment to build reading skills. A child who does not speak English may certainly recognize the sign of a McDonald's restaurant.

Visual and Performing Arts

- Let the children help make the outdoor area beautiful. Hang their paintings on the fence or have them make sculptures to decorate the fence posts. Have conversations about what beauty means and how it makes us feel. This can be a valuable outlet for self-expression for DLL children.
- Plant flowers just because they look pretty. Talk about taking care of the environment so that everyone can enjoy it.
- Designate an outdoor "stage," bring out some dress-up clothes and props, and see how the children express themselves through dancing and singing. Finding new ways to encourage communication among the children who are not fluent in English can be an eye-opening experience for teachers.

Family Connections

- Go a step beyond asking parents or family members to come in and read to children in their home language. Ask them to come during outdoor time and teach the whole class some of the chants or games they enjoyed playing when they were young.
- Instead of the usual parent and family member workshop, plan a nature day with a picnic on the playground so parents and family members can understand the learning experiences that take place outdoors so they can support that learning at home in their children's home languages.

Classroom Technology Tips

- Laminate digital photo reminders of the safety rules and post them at the appropriate locations throughout the outdoor play area.
- Use email or your program's website to start an idea-sharing network with other teachers in your program or in neighboring programs to learn new games, resources, and ideas for fun outdoor activities that can extend learning for all children.

Questions for Teacher Reflection

- Were you able to duplicate some of your own childhood learning experiences for the children in your class? How can you differentiate that learning for the language needs of each child? How can you document that differentiation?
- How can you find some of your favorite childhood books about the outdoors and recreate them in different languages so all of the children can enjoy them?
- Does your current curriculum provide specific guidance that will help you support DLLs? If not, have you adapted it so that your instruction reaches all children?

Library/ Reading Area

Think about...

- Every issue of *Young Children* magazine includes a "Book Chair" article that offers fresh ideas about reading for teachers to consider. Talk with your colleagues about how the suggestions might be modified to address different languages.

- Visit the website www.colorincolorado.org and bring some literacy suggestions for your colleagues to consider.

- Think of your favorite book to read to the children. Is it the same as your colleagues' favorite books? Take some time to think about why you love that book or why you feel it is so effective—and use this understanding to guide your choices of books for children in different languages.

- How many opportunities during the day you have to be a "reading role model"? Catch yourself reading during the school day and think of ways to increase attention to your own enjoyment of reading.

- How does your current curriculum address reading with DLL children?

The library area of any preschool classroom can be a vital and wonderful place. High-quality classrooms offer at least two books per child, and teachers rotate some of the books regularly to keep things interesting. Favorite books, like old friends, should always be there. It is important to make sure a significant number of the books in the library area are high-quality books that reflect the home languages and cultures of all of the children in your classroom. Especially with young dual language learners, the selection of the right books reinforces the value of their home language, shows respect for their culture, and has a positive impact on their identity and self-esteem. Think carefully about the selection of books for your library. Books about TV characters may catch children's attention but rarely offer sufficient learning value. Look for authentic books from different countries and cultures. Ask your language advisory committee (see page 22) to review each book to make sure it is appropriate.

Selecting Books for a Class Library

Books in different languages help to introduce and reinforce themes, concepts, words, letters, and sounds for each language. It is not enough to have books on a shelf. Teachers must use those books effectively (Meier, 2004). Children need to talk about the books and think about the meaning of the stories. All children need to hear stories in their home languages, but they can also benefit from lively story reading in other languages. Find your inner actor. Don a silly hat. Use funny voices. Make the story come alive using facial expressions, gestures, emotional tones, and body language.

Bilingual books can help children from other language backgrounds learn English, and they can help English-speaking children learn the languages of their friends. In addition, the simple language and pictures in storybooks can help teachers and volunteers learn the languages of the children in the classroom. However, remember that translations are not always identical in content.

Here's an example from a well-known storybook, *Love You Forever* by Robert Munsch and translated to French by Robert Paquin.

The beautiful refrain in English says:
I'll love you forever,
I'll like you for always,
As long as I'm living,
My baby you'll be.

Equally beautiful, the French version says:
Je t'aimerai toujours,
La nuit comme le jour;
Et tant que je vivrai,
Tu seras mon bebe.

(The second line means "the night like the day," rather than "I'll like you for always," so the author kept the poetic appeal of the passage instead of making a word-for-word translation that may have been less beautiful.)

The book area should have a focus and an identity. Program administrators who use the ECERS-R as a guide offer soft furnishings and plenty of books so children and adults feel comfortable lingering and enjoying the books throughout the day. Other classrooms that just have a few books on a shelf or in a box on the side of the classroom do not see much traffic in the book area. Stuffed animals, a soft rug, bean bag, or other low comfy chairs really do make a difference in this area of the classroom.

Books in Action

Once you have selected key books according to your curriculum, create a book plan for the week based on your learning goals and themes. Encourage bilingual staff or volunteers to talk about the book of the week with individual children or small groups in their home languages to help them become familiar with its story and characters. Read the book to the whole group several times over several days (if they seem to like it) so they can all learn the story and the words in case they want to "read" it themselves.

Vary the way you read a book: Sometimes, read the book straight through so that the children can fully enjoy the beauty of the words and pictures as the author intended. Other times, "talk" the book more than read it to engage children in learning, speculation, and conversation. Use the hints below to modify these strategies to reach the bilingual children in your class. Determine what works with the children in your class and just dive right in, knowing that you can change strategies as necessary.

Research on reading development for older grades shows a distinction between word level skills and text level skills. Many studies (August and Shanahan 2008) have shown that Latino children who attended preschool may enter kindergarten with word level skills (alphabet knowledge, letter sounds) similar to their English monolingual peers. However, as they get older, the achievement gap widens due to differences in text level skills (understanding the content of what they are reading).

The Inside Story

NAEYC recommends that preschool programs with dual language learners should increase their attention to content learning. Knowing the alphabet and word sounds is important, but should not take the place of learning about the meaning of a story. Instead of taking the time to point out the author and illustrator every time you read, use that time to ask more questions about what might happen and how the characters might feel or behave.

Take some time to visit other classrooms during their story times. Think about the different styles you see and watch the reactions of the children. All of our acting abilities and the things we do to enhance book reading really do make such a difference to children who are just beginning to learn English. A variety of strategies can bring those books to life for young dual language learners.

The Classroom Environment

Consider the following ideas for making the classroom environment welcoming for all children:

- Buy books in the languages of your students—and the community. Use a Home Language Survey to find out the home countries of your DLL children to find books that represent their culture. If all of your Spanish books refer to country life, children from San Juan may not relate to those books even if they are in the home language.
- Use your public library and your librarians as resources. Not only does this save money, but the librarians will know what languages are in your community and may have sources for books and translations that you don't know about.
- Set up a cozy reading area that encourages all children to seek out books, and make sure adults are available to enjoy all the benefits of books with them when they seem interested.
- Make key word labels for the books written in English. Highlight some key words in the children's home languages so you or another reader can say those words when using the book with small groups or individual children.
- Make sure there are appropriate books in all classroom areas. Some of those books should be written in the home language of each child in the classroom.
- Offer a wide variety of types of books in the languages of each child in the class: fiction, nonfiction, poetry, silly books, books with predictable refrains that children can repeat, traditional stories, modern stories, alphabet books, and books about the cultures of the children.
- Add props to the reading area that will help DLL children enjoy and understand stories, such as puppets from the stories, flannel boards, and writing supplies so they can write their own stories.
- Support the learning that happens with books by extending those props to other areas of the classroom. If you have added a collection of books about transportation, find an old steering wheel for the block area, some astronaut and bus driver outfits for dramatic play, and some small cars for the manipulative area.

Language Enhancement Activities

Consider the following ideas for making classroom activities welcoming for all children:

- Compile prop boxes for some of the children's favorite books. Some teachers set these up and then keep them in a central location so they can be shared throughout the program. For example, a prop box for "Goldilocks and the Three Bears" might have that picture book in English and the other languages spoken in the classroom; a curly blond wig; porridge bowls in three sizes; three bear-nose masks; a CD of bear-themed songs; a tape measure to measure small, medium and large; pretend play items like a hat for baby bear, a tie for papa bear, and an apron for mama bear; and a small blanket and pillow.

- Give each child a prop to hold or a role to play. This helps children pay attention even when they don't yet understand all the words in the story.

- Reach for a book as a pictorial representation. If a child is in the kitchen area trying to tell you what he is cooking in words you don't understand, go get the book about cooking from the library area and ask the child to point to the items he wants to talk about.

- Use books to set up themes over time. Collecting a number of books that feature a key word or just a few words, such as a group of books about bears, creates small and manageable themes.

- Avoid simultaneous translations. If you read a sentence in the child's home language and then read the sentence in another language, children will tend to listen to the language they know and ignore the unfamiliar language. (The same thing happens with adults—try it yourself!). A better way is to use the book in one language to introduce the story and familiarize individual children or small groups with the vocabulary, then use the same book in the target language at a larger story time or at another point in the day.

- Use the Internet to network with neighboring programs to share translations, prop kits, and ideas to add variety and save money.

- Learn some basic American Sign Language (ASL) signs to illustrate in the content of the books you share with DLL children. Even better, use the signs to give cues about what is coming next in the story to help children focus, predict, and comprehend.

The Storyteller in Each of Us

What You Need	Key Words and Phrases	
A favorite storybook that can be acted out easily, such as "The Three Little Pigs" Character costumes, including hats, masks, or t-shirts, for wolf and three pigs Props to represent the flimsy straw, brittle sticks, and strong bricks Story paper for children to create their own stories	Bricks Built Chin House I'll huff and I'll puff I'll blow your house down Little Pig Sticks	Straw Strong Three Weak Wolf

What to Do

* Read the storybook to the children.
* Use the key words to prepare yourself in advance by learning them in the languages that the children speak. Ask your bilingual staff to explain the story using the key words and helping the DLL children to connect the English key words with their understanding of the story.
* Encourage children who are shy or who do not speak English to participate by inviting them to be a part of the storytelling group rather than asking them to speak independently.
* Put on the costumes and act out the story using the repeating choruses to emphasize words and letter sounds. Then discuss the story with the children. Ask them open-ended questions such as, "What makes a house strong or weak?" "What kind of house do you live in?" and, "What might happen the day after the story ends?"

Extend the Learning

* Using the language they are most comfortable with, have children tell, write, or draw what happens next in "The Three Little Pigs" story.
* Later in the day or the next day, invite children to put the costumes back on, get out the props and act out the additional stories written by the children themselves. This gives the opportunity to reinforce the vocabulary and concepts introduced in the story.
* For the DLL children, seeing their stories acted out in their own language by classmates can help them see how much their language is valued in the classroom. Help the monolingual English speakers in the class learn the words of the non-English story.

Links to Learning Standards

Math

- Find counting books in your children's home languages, and place related props nearby so children can practice independently as they go through the books.
- Make math part of the library area. If you are featuring *Cloudy with a Chance of Meatballs* by Judi Barrett, make a chart with a picture of meatballs with a smiley face on one column and a picture of meatballs and a sad face on the other, then let children write their names on the column that shows their feelings about meatballs. At the end of the day or week, you can count up the responses—letting children participate at their own level.

Science

- Provide nonfiction books in different languages about nature and how things work. If they are hard to find, ask your translation committee to help you translate key words in the nonfiction books you have, and add them to your English books with stickers.
- Use books to help build children's powers of observation by making a color copy of one of the pages, cutting the copy into smaller pieces, and have the child spy through the book until they find the page that matches the copy. This can be done with children who don't speak your language and can be made gradually more challenging with word cues as they get more advanced.

Social, Relationship, and Self-Regulation

- Connect books to your DLL children by pointing out the similarities between them and the characters. You might even substitute the child's name in the book.
- Making the time for individual reading helps the children understand that each of their classmates is valued and special and that their language matters. Chang et al. (2007) found that DLL children were less likely to be victims of bullying in classrooms where the teacher spent more time talking to them in their home language.
- Introduce bilingual books that can help children learn how to solve problems and make friends.

Language Arts and Literacy

- Help the DLL children learn words and common English phrases that they can use to communicate more easily and develop a better understanding of the language.
- A book such as *Did You Say Pears?* by Arlene Alda illustrates how words that sound the same can have different meanings. Teach listening for a purpose to help children focus their attention on listening.
- Create a feature area to place a collection that has an important element in common, for example all alphabet books one day, books with rhyming words another day, and books about bugs another day.

- If you don't speak the languages of the children in your class, practice pantomime to convey questions so the children can be encouraged to talk about books even if you don't understand everything they say.

Visual and Performing Arts

- Choose some books just for their vivid and irresistible illustrations.
- Compare books with the same illustrator to help all of the children develop visual discrimination and aesthetic sensitivity regardless of language ability.
- Contrast books by different illustrators for the same purpose.
- Put out art tools and supplies that allow children to mimic how the illustrations are made in books you are reading. Some are watercolor, some are collage, some may just be line drawings, but the active, nonverbal learning involved in art will help DLL children extend their learning.

Family Connections

- Ask parents and family members to bring books from their home countries (screen for appropriateness).
- Prepare take-home bags of home literacy materials.
- Ask parents and family members to record favorite classroom books on tape or podcast so children can listen during the day.
- Teach parents or family members and staff about cognates in English and Spanish. Cognates are pairs of words, one from one language and one from the other, that sound alike, look similar, and have very similar meanings (see box above left). Parents and family members can help their child learn the connection between English and Spanish words using cognates, which simplifies the process of transfer.

Classroom Technology Tips

- Use a digital camera to make classroom books and ask family members or volunteers to translate.
- Make color copies of some pages of books, cut out key features or characters, and glue them on felt or cardboard. Use these small props to show a DLL child the role of that character or feature in the story.

Questions for Teacher Reflection

- Did you consider what makes a book your favorite or why you feel it is so effective? How can this understanding guide your choices of books for DLL children?
- Are you a "reading role model'" for the children in your classroom?
- How does your current curriculum address reading with DLLs?

Small Toy/ Manipulative Area

Think About...

* Consider the learning objectives you have planned for the small toy area of your classroom. Where else in the classroom can you find opportunities to address those same objectives so you can capture that learning wherever the child may be showing interest?

* Carry around a notepad for a day and note any realistic activity in your life that involves sorting, estimating, counting, one-to-one corresponding, comparing, and so on. At the end of the day, think about how you can incorporate more real-life examples of math and fine motor coordination into the small toy area.

* How can you be more systematic about noting each child's interests? This knowledge is key to planning differentiated instruction that will be effective and long-lasting.

The small toy area is the perfect location for many activities and materials that are customized to provide differentiated learning experiences that you design to meet the needs of each child. When a child shows an interest in sitting down and concentrating on a table activity, you can be sure that she is ready for a conversation about that activity. Labels and contents in this area come from the curriculum, the early childhood education culture in a particular community, or the preferences of the teachers and administrators. Sometimes, these areas are called "manipulatives," "small toys," "table toys," "puzzles," "math," and "game" areas. No matter what you call it, this is a great place to sit down and have some one-on-one or small-group interactions with the DLL children in your classroom. If you speak their home languages, this is a great time to have home language conversations. If you do not speak their home languages, the presence of so many objects that are easy to manipulate will enhance the communication attempts between you and your DLL children.

Developmentally Appropriate Learning

Many teachers use the manipulatives area to concentrate on math concepts. Math is an important component of the discussion about achievement gaps between white children and Latino children, and it appears as an area where U.S. children lag behind children in many other countries (The Education Trust, 2008).

Educators agree that the best place to start improving America's math competence is with the youngest children. However, preschool educators must strongly resist efforts to bring "big kid" work into the world of preschool. We have to uphold developmentally appropriate practices for preschool, and we have to make special efforts to reach diverse learners with math learning. Keeping preschool class sizes small is very important to allow teachers to achieve that balance between allowing children to have some time for independent exploration and play, and to intervene to enhance and document learning wherever it happens.

Intentional Teaching

Simply offering children baskets of connecting blocks and puzzles does not guarantee that children, especially DLLs, will learn the math concepts they need. A child who is quietly absorbed in playing with Lego© blocks or Tinker Toys© is easy to overlook in a busy classroom. You must make it a priority to observe and document children's learning. In addition, try to be more intentional in shaping the math learning that occurs in a well-stocked small toy area.

In a monolingual English class, you might get a little teaching in by making comments as you pass by the small toy table on your way to another activity. With dual language learners, however, you may not know if these brief comments have any effect at all. Talking children through the learning that happens in this area requires a greater depth of intentionality with bilingual children to make sure they understand the interesting things they are accomplishing with small toys.

The small toy/manipulatives area is a good place to gather anecdotes to add to portfolios for performance-based assessments. Assessing children's learning requires focusing on what is happening during children's play. Because bilingual children will not be able to express all of their learning in English (of course, that may be true of many preschool children, even English monolinguals), having plenty of opportunities for them to show what they know and understand is even more important.

The Classroom Environment

Consider the following ideas for making the classroom environment welcoming for all children:

- ☀ Replace some of the generic plastic stacking/building/ sorting toys with collections of real items such as buttons, bottle caps, stones, or dominoes that can be sorted, counted, stacked, strung, and used for counting games.
- ☀ Label the toy containers with all relevant languages in their assigned colors and with pictures.
- ☀ Post signs or placemats showing how the children can use the toys. A child who has never played with dominoes may not readily notice that they can be used for matching games as well as for building and racing (standing up a series of dominoes on end then knocking one down so it knocks the next which knocks the next—causing a "domino race").
- ☀ Swap out some of the manipulatives periodically to include items that support classroom themes. For example, if you are working on projects related to the post office, you might introduce a collection of postcards to this area and use them for counting and sorting activities and games. This allows the DLL children to work on math skills within the supportive context of vocabulary they have already learned from classroom theme talk.
- ☀ Taking this approach a step further, think about including items in the small toy area to prepare children for an upcoming field trip. For example, bring out a collection of little farm animals before taking a trip to a local farm. While playing with those items at the table, use the opportunity to converse about farms in the child's home language and introduce some of the words in English to lay the groundwork for the upcoming trip.

Language Enhancement Activities

Consider the following ideas for making classroom activities welcoming for all children:

- Create "conversation buddies" by pairing children who speak the same language (Dragan, 2005). This area can be a great place for them to play together and use their best language to talk about what they are doing.

- Create simple games to teach concepts. Using a standard game format, children who are unfamiliar with the English language will get to know how to play the game. Then you can switch the board and pieces to add to their learning based on the rules and procedures they've already learned. For example: Teach children to roll a die and move the game piece the number of dots they count on the die. Begin with a cube that only has two numbers on it, and then build to higher or different numbers or use colors or pictures. Another option is to create a game board that shows progressions that fit into your theme, such as the stages of growth of a plant when the children are studying plants.

- Invite the children to help you make labels for the items and containers in the manipulatives area using photos, tracings, and vocabulary in English and other classroom languages.

- Use photos of the children for sorting and counting activities. Sort by boys versus girls, shirt colors, or whatever is notable. This type of activity also helps DLL children learn the names of their classmates.

Memory Game

What You Need	Key Words
A blank game board	All done
A set of small photos that are part of the children's environment and illustrate concepts or vocabulary you want the children to learn. Glue these on cardboard or laminate them.	Face down
	Game
	Match
	Memory
	No match
Small toys that represent the items in the photos	Pick two
	Pictures
Podcast of the names of each item in the pictures in English and all relevant languages, loaded onto your computer or mp3 player	Turn over
	the names of all the objects in the photos

What to Do

- ☀ Set out the photos in rows.
- ☀ Allow each child to turn over two photos at a time to see if they match.
- ☀ Talk about the pictures quite a bit to build vocabulary about items that have strong meaning for the children.

Extend the Learning

- ☀ Once children are experts at this memory game format, you can use any set of digital photographs to increase depth and variety.
- ☀ Use the format of the game to build on children's prior knowledge and also help them learn the concepts or vocabulary represented.
- ☀ Use this game as a structure to learn key words for your next theme, or to learn a new set of materials.
- ☀ Vary the game by introducing the podcast of names. Pick one language and wait to hear a word, repeat it—then look for the matching pictures.
- ☀ Another variation involves reaching into a bag and pulling out a small toy— naming it in the language you have chosen for your game—and then looking for the matching pictures.

Links to Learning Standards

Math

* Choose counting items with a purpose. For example, count out crayons or paper to make sure there is enough for everyone. Count out four wheels if you want the children to build a model car that will move. Making the activity more realistic will help your DLL children make the proper connections.

* Sort items that would normally have to be sorted at home. Develop a collection of costume jewelry sets from yard sales—and use them for sorting and matching. Bring in a box of socks to sort for the same purpose (connecting to real life and reducing the new vocabulary demand of the sorting activity, and so the sorting concepts can be the focus).

* An excellent sorting activity is right under your nose: clean-up time! Teachers can be more intentional with their instructions about clean-up time in the small toy area. Show DLL children exactly what is in each bin and how it is to be put away. Maybe even mix items from several bins and let them "help" you sort them for clean-up time.

* Sometimes, it can be easier to introduce one-to-one correspondence with humor and mistakes. When it is time to go outside, hand a child three mittens and watch the conversation unfold. When the child realizes that three mittens is wrong, it becomes easier to understand why two mittens is right.

* Look for shapes in real things rather than drilling DLL children on identifying abstract shapes with no real meaning. You might even go on a triangle hunt around the classroom. This adds opportunities for realistic associations and adds interest to the conversations about shapes.

Science

* Get all of your children used to asking the question, "what would happen if?" Set out samples in the manipulatives area and test the children's questions by demonstrations that DLL children can understand.

* Don't just play with the small toys, examine their properties. Which ones feel smooth or rough? Which ones snap or stick together and why? What are they made of? In this way, through demonstration, you can teach children to be more careful observers of their immediate environment regardless of their language.

Social, Relationship, and Self-Regulation

* Play start/stop games, which are easy to demonstrate for DLL children. For example, have children start puzzles, and then ring a bell signaling they should stop and move to the next person's puzzle and take over. This type of activity gives children the experience of self regulation.

* Encourage peer-to-peer conversation. For example, if a dual language learner shows that she needs help to open some playdough or fit a puzzle piece into a puzzle, invite another child in the area to help her.

- Narrate children's play to encourage DLL children to join in and be accepted by the other children.

Language Arts and Literacy

- As the DLL children gain confidence in English, pair a new bilingual child with a child more adept in English so their interactions can help the newer learner to build English skills and help the more expert children celebrate their own abilities.
- Learn how to say, "Show me" or Show me how" in each child's home language. As the child learns that you will help communication by pointing to the items, gesturing, signing, or miming, the child can learn to show you what she is talking about in the same way. Table toy play is fun, and with shared language it is even better.
- Confirm children's English vocabulary learning by setting up an I Spy game for a small group. Put a few objects on the table that you think they can name in English. Then ask them to say which item answers your question, such as, "Which toy is red?" "Which one is round?" or "Which is the biggest?" By combining children's established vocabulary with additional words they are learning, you can expand the connections they make as they learn words and concepts.

Visual and Performing Arts

- Provide materials to make small-scale sculptures. This is a great medium for self-expression for children who are struggling with language.
- Focus on how things look in terms of balance, pattern, and attractiveness. This helps DLL children begin to see these elements in their own work as they learn to use descriptive words.

Family Connections

- Ask parents and family members to have their children bring sorting items from home, such as buttons, bottle caps, clean egg cartons, or acorns. Children take pride in talking about the items that they bring in from their homes. Use this opportunity to inform parents and family members about the many chances for learning that occur at home.
- Ask the children's families to send in games from their home countries.
- A parent or family member who is hesitant to read aloud or sing songs with the children may be more inclined to show some children how to play traditional children's games from her culture.

Classroom Technology Tips

- Use a digital camera to take photographs of your class and surrounding area. Download and print them, and then paste the photos on cardboard. Cut the cardboard into puzzles. The children love to talk about these "personal" puzzles. If children are young and still require simple wooden puzzles, consider tracing your photos on old puzzles and gluing the photos on the existing pieces. Then hammer on small spools or large beads to use as handles on the puzzle pieces.
- Create pattern-matching cards with photos of the real items you have on hand (each card shows a pattern you want the child to repeat such as black button, white button, white button, black button, white button, white button). This allows you to differentiate instruction by targeting the complexity of the task to each child's needs.

Questions for Teacher Reflection

School districts, Head Start programs, and preschools often have a variety of experts at their disposal to help preschool teachers. For example, ESL teachers in a school district may have expertise to share about meeting the needs of DLLs. Because pull-out or push-in ESL strategies are often too short-term and too disruptive to be effective with preschool children, the K–12 ESL teacher's expertise would be better used in consultation with the classroom teacher. Reflective questions like those below will help to structure the consultative interactions between the ESL specialist and the classroom teacher.

- How can the ESL teacher learn more about developmentally appropriate practice and about your preschool curriculum? What are key points you want that consulting teacher to understand?
- What did you observe in other areas in the classroom that address the same objectives as those in the small toy area?
- Are you planning to incorporate more real-life examples of math and fine motor coordination into the small toy area? How?
- How will you provide differentiated instruction that will be effective and long-lasting?

Writing Area

Think About...

- Consider keeping a journal. Just as teachers encourage children in preschool to keep journals, your own writing can be an effective strategy for reflective teaching.

- Look up your state's early learning standards related to writing and think about how you are meeting those standards specifically with dual language learners (DLL). As you think more creatively and deeply about meeting the needs of bilingual children in preschool, how might you change those standards to address the true needs and abilities you observe?

- Find out which labels the children notice and use in the classroom. Think about ways you could vary the labels or draw new attention to them.

- How often do children see you writing for a purpose? How often do DLL children see adults writing in their home languages? How can everyone be more intentional in showing the important role of writing in our everyday lives?

It may seem overwhelming to focus on writing when the DLL children in the classroom are just beginning to understand their new language. But that is exactly why we must focus on developing writing skills. Too often, teachers put off this aspect of preschool learning for bilingual children during the time when it is developmentally important for all children. The strategies in this chapter help children progress with both the fine-motor aspects of writing as well as the aspects of writing that connect to pre-reading skills.

More than Meets the Eye

Much more than simply practicing writing goes on in the writing area. All of the models you provide for beginning writers can relate to themes and projects in the classroom. The writing area can be full of items that connect to each child's culture and language, and can provide the children with a unique opportunity to share their thoughts and feelings.

It is important not to try to force writing activities. Certainly, writing is an important precursor to reading (Strickland and Schickedanz, 2004), but as this book goes to print, there is no significant research that shows any value in accelerating the teaching of writing skills before children are developmentally ready. Many developmental aspects to the acquisition of writing ability are not entirely under the control of the preschool teacher or the child.

Vast individual differences in writing ability exist among three- and four-year-old children. These differences are influenced by development of fine motor coordination and strength, cognitive development, perceptual abilities, and each child's interest in the acts of pre-writing and writing. Uncertainty with the home language and/or the new language can add another layer of complexity to this area of development. Forcing a child who is not interested in writing or who is not developmentally ready to pursue it will only get in the way of this learning goal. Think of it this way: You could try to force a two-year-old child to practice riding a two-wheeler with no training wheels over and over for hours every day until he finally learns how to ride. Or you could wait until the child is developmentally ready, then show him how in just a few hours. Sure, every child should learn to ride a bicycle, but what do you gain by starting too early?

Generally, programs that devote inordinate amounts of time to a curriculum for a specific skill are trying to teach a skill that is not developmentally appropriate for the children. If something is that hard to teach, it is too soon to teach it. The best way to learn about print is to observe it and practice it wherever it might occur naturally. This is especially true for preschool dual language learners who must struggle with the challenge of learning about writing while they are also confronted with struggles to learn content.

Follow the Child's Lead

It is developmentally appropriate to expose preschool children of all languages to the concept of writing, give them plenty of opportunities to see writing in action, and allow them to try it themselves. Certainly, any child who likes to practice writing should be encouraged to do so. Follow each child's lead and write lesson objectives for each individual child. If a child comes to the writing area but is not ready to write, consider just playing letter recognition games with him. Each child should feel fully accepted and respected in the writing area and be able to see writing models in his home language.

Writing is part of the overall literacy component of concepts of print. When planning writing opportunities for bilingual children, be sure to address the following related areas:

- The connection between writing and meaning. For DLL children keep it as real as possible.
- The meaning of words. What is a word? Match words to speech and to images on a page with spaces between.
- The direction of print. Do children in your classroom speak languages that are read from right to left? Discuss this with all of the children.
- Alphabet knowledge. Ideally, preschoolers should learn the alphabet of their home language first. This gives them a firm foundation in letter knowledge that is easy to transfer to English when they get older.
- Phonemic awareness. Children can learn the sounds of letters that make up words in their home language first. Research (August and Shanahan, 2008) shows this transfers easily to a second language as long as it is learned well in the first.

The Classroom Environment

Consider the following ideas for making the classroom environment welcoming for all children:

- Children from all language backgrounds should have a fun and engaging area to explore and practice writing in the form they see at home as well as in English.
- Include models of the different kinds of writing that reflect the cultures and languages in your class.
- Create word model cards that can stay in the writing area and that captivate every child in the class.
- Make writing fun by offering a variety of papers in different colors, sizes, and textures.
- Offer a variety of writing implements that represent different cultures such as calligraphy brushes, rustic pencils, chalk, pens, and markers.
- Have writing implements available in all areas of the classroom to capitalize on DLL children's interest in writing whenever they think of it.

- Provide alphabet books as well as blocks, tiles, and magnets showing the proper alphabet for the languages in your classroom.
- Make sure functional print, such as handwashing instructions, rules for safe outdoor play, or organizational labels in the music area, is visible at children's eye level. Change labels often to draw attention to them. Include all classroom languages as well as illustrative pictures or photos.

Language Enhancement Activities

Consider the following ideas for making classroom activities welcoming for all children:

- Use story dictation with a twist: Write whatever the child says in whatever language he says it. Switching between languages is normal. As a scribe, it is important to write what you hear, even if you do not know the exact spelling of the foreign word. You can ask children's family members or look up unfamiliar words later.
- Be obvious in pointing out print everywhere in the classroom.
- Arrange a word hunt: Hand out cards with single words that clearly match words in the environmental print throughout the room or beyond. Encourage the children to match them with the environmental print in the classroom.
- Find opportunities to post each child's name. This is especially important for a DLL child who may feel lost or almost invisible in a group that doesn't speak his language.
- Be intentional about scaffolding writing skills. If a DLL child recognizes his own name at his cubby, then introduce a new challenge, such as picking out his name from the set of attendance cards, then writing his name on the attendance sheet, and so on.
- Show children how much you value writing. Write notes, reminders, questions, and anything else that seems useful, making an effort to draw their attention to the usefulness of writing. If you are sitting with a preschool bilingual child who is slowly working on copying words to "write" a note to his mom, you might "suddenly" remember that you want to write a note to your own mom at the same time.
- Learn more about shared writing. A wonderful way for uncertain DLLs to be part of the writing action is to recreate a description of a shared experience. Write down everything the children say on poster sheets. Enhance their understanding by adding drawings or pictures clipped from magazines. Shared writing where a bilingual teacher switches between two languages is especially good for DLL children. It can help children see that words they know and words their friends know come together and share meaning when they are talking about the same topic.

Writing from Home

What You Need	Key Words	
Ask family members to provide writing models in their home languages.	Aunt	Mom
	Cousin	Note
	Dad	Post office
Send home a list of words or topics and ask family members to write them out in their home language on word cards.	Envelope	School
	Grandma	Stamp
	Grandpa	Uncle
	House	Write
Collect digital photos or magazine pictures to illustrate the chosen words.	Letter	Writing
	Mail	
	Mailbox	

What to Do

* Invite the children to write notes in their home languages.

* Use the family members' word models so the children can see the handwriting their family members use at home and make the connection between that and the learning they are doing at home.

* Find out how the family members refer to themselves and to the child. Knowing whether to call his mother "mama," "maman," or "mommy" will help you bond with a DLL child as he attempts to write a note home. This added support can boost the child's confidence.

Extend the Learning

* Take the children on a field trip to the post office so they can see how letters are processed.
* Expand the post office theme to the whole classroom if it captures the children's interest.
* Count letters and compare sizes and shapes.
* Use the family members' word models in other areas of the classroom as applicable.
* Work with the children's familes to help the children send letters to their relatives in other countries.

Links to Learning Standards

Math

* Make response charts available in the writing area. Ask children to write in their responses to a question that can be shown with illustrations, and use it to encourage counting. In the beginning, response charts might ask only that the child make a mark in the column of their choice so all children can participate and see the value of beginning writing. Make sure the choices are shown in words and in pictures to be clear for all language speakers.

* Have the children "write" their favorite recipes in their home languages. This is great writing experience, of course, but it also demonstrates the value numbers have in our writing.

Science

* Teach children how to use writing to take observation notes in their science notebooks and offer word cards in the appropriate languages to get them started.

* Explore the properties of the things people use for writing. What happens when you write on rough art paper, as opposed to smooth fingerpaint paper? What happens to marker ink when you drop water on it? How is that different than what happens when you drop water on crayon writing or pencil writing? Can you erase pencil marks, ink marks, or crayon marks? Why? This strategy allows you to provide additional support for the vocabulary behind writing activities for your DLL children and emphasize the importance of this important literacy skill in a way that children of varying language levels can enjoy.

Social, Relationship, and Self-Regulation

* Journaling can be especially important for DLL children as a way to focus on their attempts at written language without the pressure of doing it "right."

* Early writing is a chance for DLL children to express their thoughts and feelings while they are not yet adept or confident at spoken language. It also gives you a chance to capture learning portfolio samples to evaluate (and translate, if need be) at some other time.

Language Arts and Literacy

* Scrutinize the posters, bulletin boards, puzzles, and game pieces you have around the classroom to serve as writing models. Are they truly appropriate for young children, and are they specifically appropriate for the cultures and backgrounds of the children in your class? For example, we often see the letter "A" illustrated by an anchor. How many preschool children have actually seen an anchor? And even if they have, it probably did not look like the stylized anchors we see in posters or language assessments. Further, children use many kinds of "sleds" to slide down hills in the snow, but how many children use those old traditional sleds made out of wood and metal? Yet, we still see them used in writing and early literacy sample items. It would be better to use airplane for "A" or a slide for the "Sl" sound.

- Watch out for unclear or ambiguous pictures. Learning letters and sounds in another language is hard enough without a lot of trick questions. For example, a picture of an iguana may depict the letter "I." However, children may call it a lizard instead.

Visual and Performing Arts

- Read authentic, original poetry from the languages and cultures of the children, and be prepared to act out the poetry to bring its meaning to life and to add spice to writing activities. This will prepare the children to try acting out their own writings, enriching the overall experience of writing.
- Writing practice should focus on more than basic alphabet letters and words. Have models and supports available to help DLL children try to write with flare about their own artwork or their own stories. Beautifully illustrated books or brochures in home languages, or word cards with interesting vocabulary words are some examples.

Family Connections

- Ask the children's family members to prepare writing models in their own handwriting so children can connect their learning, and so the family members can have more ownership of their contribution to children's prewriting and pre-literacy development.
- Find out if any of the family members of the children in your class are involved in adult education ESL classes. This can be a great source of collaboration that benefits both children and adults. Maybe the family members can practice writing in English and make writing models for children. Or the family members and children can practice their writing by being pen pals.

Classroom Technology Tips

- Search the Internet for signs, images, or even book covers on www.amazon.com to print out useful words in the children's home languages.
- Use the Internet to look up words in different languages to illustrate letters of the alphabet for writing cues. Don't use an apple for the letter "Aa"; in Spanish apple is "una manzana." But, you might use a "boat" for the letter "Bb" because the Spanish word is "el barco," and the French is "le bateau."
- Find computer software or websites, such as www.babelfish.yahoo.com/ that give you the sounds of words in other languages so you can say the words correctly as you help the DLL child write in his home language.
- Many children's software packages are designed to help preschoolers learn keyboard literacy and traditional literacy skills, such as letter recognition, print awareness, and phonemic awareness. Look for programs available in the home languages of your children. Be cautious about purchasing software. Make sure it truly fits your curriculum and is developmentally appropriate. Just because a

program comes in Spanish does not mean it will help your children learn. Look for ease of use and opportunities for children to learn actively and creatively. Software must not take the place of teaching. The best children's software gets children talking and thinking.

Questions for Teacher Reflection

How has your own journal writing helped you to think more deeply about your strategies for supporting DLL children in your class?

- Does your state have early learning standards for preschool children? Look up the standards related to writing and think about how you are meeting those standards, specifically with regard to DLL children.

- As you think more creatively and deeply about meeting the needs of bilingual children in preschool, how might you change those standards to address the true needs and abilities you observe?

- Did you identify new ways to vary the environmental print in your classroom or draw new attention to it? How might you share your new ideas with colleagues?

- Have you begun to point out your actions to the children when you write for a purpose? How have the children responded?

- How can everyone be more intentional in showing the role of writing in our everyday lives?

Science Area

Think About...

☀ Think back to your earliest memory of having fun with science. Was it exploring outdoors? Getting your first pet? Helping your mom bake a cake? How can you bring the fun back into your own science teaching in preschool so you can feel confident teaching children from different language backgrounds?

☀ How can you modify your lesson plan forms to include science goals and objectives tailored to meet the needs of your diverse language learners?

☀ Think of a problem that really stumped you recently. How could science have helped you solve it? What kinds of science do you wish you knew more about? Let that realization lead you to select science concepts that children can really connect with in your class.

The science area of the classroom is particularly rich in opportunities for both concept learning and language practice that can support transitions between languages. Science is a natural interest area for young children because everything is new and fascinating to them. While it is a good idea to have a designated science area, teachers can find science discovery and curiosity almost anywhere in the classroom. The key to fostering the growth of preschool science learning is to capture those teachable moments to build on each child's unique interests rather than trying to plan large-group lessons that may have limited impact, especially in a linguistically diverse classroom.

Instead of large-scale science demonstrations for all the children in the class, consider planning learning goals that can address each child according to her needs and interests. For example, if your lesson plan calls for teaching about living things, make it your goal to talk about or demonstrate this topic with each child in your classroom at some point during the week. That may mean showing a few children the similarities and differences between twigs and caterpillars out on the playground, or reading an animal baby book in Spanish to some of the children, or asking the bilingual aide to chat with a particular child about comparing a stuffed animal with the classroom's pet guinea pig.

Science Builds Competence in Preschoolers

Preschool children enjoy science because they love the feeling of competence that comes with truly understanding something and being able to share that knowledge with others. Competence is something we especially want to foster in our new DLL children. You may teach many interesting things during the school day, but it is often the science discovery that children will chatter about when their parents and family members arrive at the end of the school day. Because science concepts make such a significant impression on children, they are valuable topics to foster deep understanding. With this deep understanding comes a strong connection with vocabulary that will strengthen children's preparation for academic learning both in English and in their home language.

Preschool teachers should receive plenty of support to develop the confidence necessary to make science a bigger part of the day. Too often, teachers have unpleasant memories of a high school or college science course that made them feel inadequate or disinterested. Instead of thinking about your grown-up experiences with science learning, try thinking about what science means to young children. For them, science starts with the most basic questions about how things work, how things change, how things are made, and how living things live and grow. As a teacher, you do not have to be a physicist, but you do have to be a fellow explorer with the children in your classroom, letting their curiosity lead the way.

Teamwork and Shared Experiences

The science area is a great place for teamwork. Children who share a language can converse about all the interesting things in the science area. Children who do not speak the same language can still explore and learn together if they learn to communicate with a peer who speaks a different language. Explain to children that it is best to speak slowly and clearly and to show what they mean by using gestures and pointing to things. Remind them they do not have to shout, but they can repeat words to help their friends understand. You may also need to remind them to really listen to their friends and allow time for the other children to think of answers to questions. Some preschool children who have younger brothers and sisters already know how to do this. They just need further coaching to understand that they already have the skills to communicate with their friends who speak different languages.

This kind of coaching helps the English-speaking children be more understanding toward their non-English speaking peers and helps the DLL children learn how to make the most out of their attempts to interact with the monolinguals. Teaching all of the children these strategies demonstrates that all of the children have strengths in language and all are responsible for helping their peers.

The Classroom Environment

Consider the following ideas for making the classroom environment welcoming for all children:

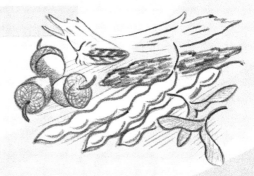

- ☀ Have collections of real items rather than store-bought science kits to ensure that learning can be built upon DLL children's prior knowledge.

- Take a tour of the science area to acquaint all the children with what is there and how to use the tools and materials.
- Ask families to send in requested science items. When they come from home, the DLL children will relate to them more clearly.
- Make sure there are living things in your room, and make sure you and the children care for and discuss them in all languages.
- Make sure there are plenty of science things to explore, then support DLL children by making sure to label these science-related items in the children's home languages, and that there are plenty of pictures to show what to do with the various items and activities.
- Keep bilingual non-fiction books available in the science area in all needed languages to illustrate and provide depth.

Language Enhancement Activities

Consider the following ideas for making classroom activities welcoming for all children:

- Think of activities that you can demonstrate using little or no language. Once you have a plan so that children can learn without spoken language, you can be sure that children are likely to learn the concepts you are conveying no matter what their language ability. Then, add to the learning by using clear but increasingly rich vocabulary in home languages and/or English to enhance the learning experience. All of the following activities address the five senses.

  - Encourage the children to use their senses of smell. Give them scented cotton balls stored in sandwich bags or small film roll containers. Chart each child's reaction using happy/sad face indicators. Bring added realism that will help DLL children connect to prior learning by filling plastic bags with smelling samples like a cut onion, a rose, or some orange sections.
  - Demonstrate the sense of touch by making texture boards. Try to incorporate textures related to your themes. For example, for a theme on planting, have cups of different types of soil or different textured leaves or bark.
  - Collect recordings or actual items to use for sound identification games.
  - Teach children how to use the magnifying glass or light table to learn about how vision works.

Absorb / Don't Absorb

What You Need

Plastic bag
Aluminum foil
Plastic lid from
   coffee can or
   similar
Tissue
Paper napkins
Paper towel
Cotton ball
Cloth towel

Banana
Bread
Books about the
   absorbent
   properties of
   different
   substances in
   all languages
Sponge

Key Words

Absorb	Paper
Banana	Plastic
Bread	Repel
Cloth	Soak
Does not absorb	Sponge
Does not soak	Water
Metal	

What to Do

❀ Spill some water and make a fuss about how you will clean it up. This is a chance for your inner comedian to come out.

❀ Try some of the items on the list that will NOT help soak up the water. While doing so, repeat several of the vocabulary words. Intentionally repeat the question, "What will absorb the water?"

❀ Try some of the absorbent materials. Discuss what is happening and why. If you are bilingual, you can do this in more than one language. If not, you will have to rely on the strong non-verbal components of this demonstration to help all of the children understand the concept of absorption.

❀ Ask, "Why do we need to know which materials will absorb a spill?" "How are bread and a banana different?" This type of authentic exploration is very effective.

Extend the Learning

❀ Invite children to play with similar test items in the water table. Supply relevant word models in the classroom languages along with photos to help children write in their science notebooks about what they observe.

❀ Place some of the materials in the dramatic play area so children of all languages can reinforce their science learning in the context of role-playing.

❀ In the manipulatives area, ask children to count how many cotton balls it takes to soak up an ounce or two of colored water in a small cup.

❀ Talk about absorb/non-absorb in the art area when you observe that watercolors soak into plain paper but roll off an area that a child colored with wax crayon, or see that water soaks into wet clay, but dried or fired clay does not let water through.

❀ Role-play a rainy day by using a spray bottle to see what happens when it "rains" on a doll wearing a t-shirt, as compared to a doll wearing a plastic rain poncho.

Links to Learning Standards

Math

* Make counting an important part of observation activities to strengthen learning based on DLL children's prior knowledge. How many points are on each leaf? How many legs does a spider have? How many carrots can the class' guinea pig eat in a day?

* Use the real items you bring in for science inquiry to demonstrate math concepts. The more connected the items are to a child's real experience, the more you can focus on the comparison learning. Here are some examples for comparisons of small, medium, and large:

    toilet roll, paper towel roll, and wrapping paper roll

    small, medium, and large paper cups

    small, medium, and large socks

    small, medium, and large cookies

Science

* Starting with inquiry, translate important science questions into the languages of the children, or practice ways to ask those questions in English with graphic organizers to assist understanding.

* Investigation (or hypothesis testing) means trying out your ideas. Focus on demonstration techniques to bring this learning home for all of the children.

* Observation skills form a vital foundation for future learning. All children can have an enhanced learning experience when the teacher uses demonstration techniques to highlight observations. These may include, for example, physically pointing out the differences between two seashells, charting the feelings of rough and smooth textures, or making sure drawing supplies are ready when presenting some new natural materials in the science area.

Social, Relationship, and Self-Regulation

* Identify photos of emotions/feelings in English and in home languages.

* Encourage children to show how they would react to something by showing facial expressions. This is an example of everyday science as you explore the ways we use our body to communicate. At the same time, children learn to express feelings across language barriers.

* Use books, field trips, and discussions in English and other languages to teach children about the connection between classroom science activities and the role science plays in the world around them.

* Post science safety rules with pictures and the languages of the classroom. For example, create a poster showing how to handle the class pet safely, so that children can learn to interact with it independently.

Language Arts and Literacy

* Make the windows a valuable part of the learning environment. They should be clean and accessible. Try not to line the walls with shelving or pile things up on

the windowsills. Weather, traffic, neighbors, animals, and so on may be favorite and familiar topics for DLL children to talk about as they look out the window.

☀ Instead of posting a sign that says "window" in several languages, try posting words you and the children can use to talk about the world outside in their home languages such as "tree," "leaves," "squirrel," "butterfly," "truck," "policeman," "delivery," "rain," or "wind." Look for ways to reinforce this vocabulary.

Visual and Performing Arts

☀ Talk about the beauty in nature to capture previously learned vocabulary for DLLs. Mention the colors we see in nature and how they change; and how caring for the environment helps our world to stay beautiful.

☀ Capture previously learned vocabulary for DLL children by talking about the science of art. Demonstrate how different art media work, how colors can blend, how different papers feel and the different ways they accept paint, markers, chalk, and crayons.

☀ Use art to demonstrate transformations to children with different language levels. Make sculptures from different modeling compounds—store-bought or homemade—and watch how they change when left out in the air.

Family Connections

☀ Find out which children's family members have science-related jobs. Think broadly. Hairdressers use chemicals to change hair color. Family members who do not work outside the home use science when baking and cooking. Invite parents or family members to come in and talk about their work activities in their home language.

☀ Offer a science workshop. Decide what works best in your community for the different language groups. Show the children's family members how to do simple and fun science experiments at home with their children. These activities encourage rich interactions that children can share with their families using interesting vocabulary and questions.

☀ Think of interesting conversation starters to encourage conversations at home. For example, "Ask your child what she learned about bears today."

Classroom Technology Tips

☀ Kid-friendly digital cameras are now available that are easy to use even for three-year-olds. Encourage children to capture photos of things that interest them in their environment and use those photos to build science learning experiences that you can link to what DLL children already know, even if they cannot yet tell you verbally.

- Have bilingual high school or college students volunteer in your class and use their technology skills. Ask them to take digital photos or short videos of a science project and show the transformations over time. Make a PowerPoint presentation with voiceover or typed captions in the languages of the classroom. For example, show the progression from seeds to grown plants or how everyone's shadows look outside.
- Science lends itself to developmentally appropriate use of the Internet in the preschool classroom. Be prepared to look up an answer to any science question that arises; you certainly do not need to know everything. Use Google Images to find out the name of a turtle that you and the children discovered in a nearby pond. Look up the translation for the word "turtle" in the languages of your classroom. Find out how sponges are made. Be sure to talk through your search process aloud so the children can learn from the strategies you use to do your research.

Questions for Teacher Reflection

Science continues to be a topic that intimidates many preschool teachers. For this reason, active learning may be most effective to help teachers build the confidence to teach science. Lesson study is an example of an active learning strategy that can support teachers in this endeavor. Lesson study (Lewis, 2004) is a structure for teacher learning that follows research methods: They plan learning activities (lessons) together, then one teacher tries the activities while the others observe, and the teachers then come together for group reflection and revision. The websites below provide examples used by teachers in the United States and in other countries.

http://www.tc.edu/lessonstudy/lesson study.html
http://www.lesson research.net/
http://www.nsdc.org/ library/strategies/ lessonstudy.cfm

Block Area

Think About...

* Evaluate the supplies in your block area. What is missing and how can you improve that area to support learning and fun across all languages?

* Locate an article or book on block activities in preschool, such as *The Block Book* (3rd edition) by Elisabeth Hirsch, and plan with colleagues to share block ideas at the next staff meeting.

* What strategies can you use to remind yourself to have a rich, meaningful conversation with at least five turns with most or all children every day?

* How will you plan to make those conversations effective with all of the children from different language backgrounds? What professional development is needed?

The block area is fertile ground for all sorts of imaginative play, mathematical exploration, and language. With its near universal appeal, the block area can be a place where a new non-English speaker can find something to enjoy in your classroom. This chapter offers ways to use the block area to the best advantage for dual language learners (DLL).

Assessing Learning in the Block Area

The block area is an important place to assess and document learning. If a child in your class does not speak much English and speaks a language you do not understand, watch her in the block area to be sure she is engaging in developmentally appropriate activities for preschoolers. Is she able to persist in one line of play for 10 or 15 minutes? Does she seem to have a plan for sophisticated play that she is following rather than just randomly stacking a couple of blocks? Is she bringing props into her play scenarios?

Room arrangement is crucial to making block play effective. Most classroom designers suggest that the block area needs to have enough space for several children to build independently or together without conflict, and that space needs to be protected from traffic pathways and other activities in the classroom.

Keep It Down!

Research shows that excess noise can interfere with learning in preschool (Nixon, 2003) and can cause bilingual learners to have more difficulty distinguishing English speech sounds (Rogers et al., 2006). So, not only do we want children's grand buildings to survive, we also want to protect other activity areas in the classroom from the excess noise of the block area.

Dense, flat carpet squares in the block area can help control noise. Children need to be free to have fun in the block area, which sometimes means listening to a spectacular crash. In multilingual classrooms, it is even more important to allow that freedom while making it easy to hear language in other areas. If falling blocks make a sound that echoes throughout the classroom, this is a red flag that should alert you to poor acoustics. Modify the classroom as much as possible to address the problem. Use materials that absorb echoing sounds, such as drapes, rugs, and wall materials like corkboards.

The Classroom Environment

Consider the following ideas for making the classroom environment welcoming for all children:

- Full sets of blocks make it possible for children to play out their imaginative schemes. The better equipped the classroom, the more likely you will see each child reveal his true potential.
- Did you know blocks can be multicultural too? You can find block sets that represent familiar architectural shapes from different cultures, such as domes, spires, and different roof shapes. Pair these with pictures of buildings from different cultures to add richness to your block area activities.
- Offer accessories that go along with building—representing the different languages/cultures of the classroom. These include people, traffic signs, animals, and vehicles.
- Have books about building available in all appropriate languages to assist with communication. If you or the child does not know the word to express a particular concept, a book may have a picture that illustrates the concept.
- Catalogs, magazines, posters, postcards, and newspapers showing buildings and building supplies—in English or another language—can help augment language in the block area.
- Offer writing implements such as colored pencils, stencils, and large paper for map drawing, or cardboard, markers, and tape for sign making.

Language Enhancement Activities

Consider the following ideas for making classroom activities welcoming for all children:

- Demonstrate which blocks stack, which blocks roll, which blocks can stand on their own, and how to sort blocks to put them away in their labeled place. These are the kinds of concepts we might just mention in passing to an exclusively English-speaking class, but DLL children need some direct attention in their home language—or via your ESL techniques—to clarify the various concepts that are at work in the block area.
- Introduce science concepts by adding different materials to the block area, such as pieces of PVC pipe or old vacuum cleaner hoses into which marbles or even small figures can disappear and come out the other side. Also consider including carpet remnant squares and pieces of fabric that can add texture and dimension to the buildings, as well as Slinkys, marbles, and balls that can roll down different ramps made with blocks. These items expand the concepts you talk about with DLL children during block play.
- Create simple maps of the classroom or the immediate neighborhood with locations labeled in all needed languages. Place them in the block area for children to copy using blocks, and then take the map for a walk around to find the key locations they just built with blocks.

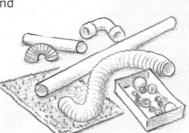

Community Walk

What You Need	Key Words	
Photos of the school building and environment, as well as key buildings in the neighborhood and other notable features such as a mailbox or street sign. For a larger building, take several photos so children can recognize its parts.	Car wash	Post Office
	Corner	School
	Deli	Sign
	Firehouse	Stop
	Front door	
	Mailbox	
Old blocks or clean milk cartons to make into blocks	Neighborhood	
	Parking lot	
Glue sticks	Pizza place	
	Playground	

What to Do

☀ Give pairs of children folders containing a few photos.

☀ Take everyone on a walk around the neighborhood.

☀ Ask the children to find buildings that match their photos, pairing same-language children so they can talk freely and build vocabulary.

☀ When you get back to the classroom, work with the children to glue the photos onto blocks that the children can then place in the block area to add depth and vocabulary to block play.

Extend the Learning

☀ Work with the children to create a class book using the photos. Let the children dictate the captions.

☀ Focus on the important science skill of observation by taking the children out on a second walk to notice what has changed since you first took the photos.

☀ Use the photos and blocks to count relevant items, such as how many windows your school has, or how many stores there are between you and the local pizza place.

☀ Build relationships between the children by emphasizing that they all share the same neighborhood and perhaps even eat at the same restaurants.

☀ Use a long photo of the street as a pattern model and see if the children can replicate the pattern of which building block belongs where. Using this representation of the DLL children's real environment enables you to build on the children's prior knowledge with any activity that uses those blocks.

Links to Learning Standards

Math

- Use unit blocks to introduce measurement with children who speak other languages. It is easier to demonstrate that your shoe is as long as seven cube blocks than it is to explain the workings of a tape measure or ruler. Once the DLL child shows understanding about lining up the blocks to count and measure, it is easy to make the connection to counting the markings on a ruler.

- For a fun comparison activity that graphically illustrates comparison, bring in some different types of paper bags: lunch bags, grocery bags, large leaf bags, or shopping bags. Have children add blocks to the bag one at a time and test the bags to see how heavy they are. Compare how heavy a bag feels with one block, three blocks, or 10. Keep adding blocks to see how many blocks it takes to rip the bag.

- To help DLL children make sense out of shape knowledge, pick up shape blocks and bring them around the room, showing the children objects in the classroom that have similar shapes.

Science

- "What would happen if...?" This is an important science question for preschoolers. There are many ways to demonstrate this question and make answers happen right before your eyes in the block area. Coach DLL children to recognize that question by adding a gesture such as the American Sign Language sign for "I wonder" to use consistently when asking this question. Then demonstrate the question at hand: Put a small, thin block on the floor, then ask, "What would happen if?" and place a larger block on top.

- Ask, "How might this change?" Teach DLL children this phrase along with the ASL sign for "change," and then role-play how things could change in the child's building. For example, use fingers or a doll to walk up to the front of the building and "wonder" how to get in. Then, help the child figure out how to add an entrance to the building.

Social, Relationship, and Self-Regulation

- Set up building teams. Pair same-language children so they can use their home language vocabulary to chatter freely about their building activities, or pair a new DLL child with a more experienced bilingual child.

- Sit on the floor and demonstrate how to take turns and work together on a building. This will help children understand how to negotiate so they can play cooperatively, even when there is a language barrier.

Language Arts and Literacy

- It is especially helpful for DLL children to build on the vocabulary they are learning elsewhere in the classroom. For example, after you read "The Three Little Pigs," add toys that look like bricks, straw, and sticks into the block area or use real-life samples of those items for a better understanding.

☀ Introduce rich and interesting vocabulary in the children's home languages. Take time to learn words like "tall," "tiny," "shaky," "enormous," and "sturdy" in the languages the children in your classroom speak.

Visual and Performing Arts

☀ Display posters of beautiful buildings and sculptures that children can copy and talk about to encourage language practice.

☀ Show children that, sometimes, you appreciate their buildings just for their artistic expression, and that they do not always need to build a "successful" structure.

Family Connections

☀ Send home messages about building with blocks and other items. Show parents and family members how children can build and sort with different sizes of cans, pots, measuring cups, and empty boxes at home, and help parents and family members think of conversation starters such as, "How can we make this taller?"

☀ Use newsletters, tipsheets, or personal conversations in the home language to help parents and family members see that the value of block play is in the imagination and the language that happens.

Classroom Technology Tips

☀ Use a digital camera to record the steps a child takes to build a building. This helps create a great addition to a child's learning portfolio, and is a great way to preserve evidence of his hard work and creativity.

☀ Take pictures of buildings in your neighborhood and glue them to blocks to make buildings more familiar and create a shared vocabulary with bilingual children. You can purchase blocks or make make blocks using cleaned, nested milk cartons and empty boxes in different sizes.

Questions for Teacher Reflection

Use the questions below to involve administrators in ongoing adaptations and planning for acquiring materials and scheduling professional development.

☀ What specific professional development does your program need to address the strategies that teachers should use to support DLL children within the program's curriculum? How has your program used data to make these decisions?

☀ Evaluate the supplies in your block area. What is missing, and how can you improve the area to support learning and fun across all languages?

☀ Are the classroom environments arranged to allow for free exploration without creating the kind of excess noise that can interfere with language learning? How can administrators help by providing articles, videos, or consultants to enhance classroom environments?

Mealtime

Think About...

- What were mealtimes like when you were growing up?
- What kinds of things did you talk about at the table? How is that similar to or different from your mealtimes now that you are an adult?
- What are some of the best things about your current and past mealtimes that you want to share with all the children in your class?

Whether it is a hot lunch or a self-serve snack, mealtime can provide opportunities for learning in every domain of preschool development. From the basic skills of sitting still and waiting for food to sophisticated understanding of how different foods affect our bodies, mealtime is a key platform for practicing necessary behavior and developing verbal skills.

Mealtime is a part of the preschool day where it is crucial to address concerns about noise. The best meals enable useful interactions. Family-style meals where teachers, assistants, and volunteers sit down with children and really talk are hallmarks of the highest quality preschool programs. Do not show videos during mealtimes. Even background music can work against the language and learning benefits of mealtimes. Nothing should distract from the rich opportunities for real, natural conversations between teachers and children, between two children who are anxious to have a chance to chatter freely in their home language, or between two children who speak different languages and want to get to know each other.

Mealtime Supports Skills Across the Curriculum

Mealtime can be a wonderful opportunity to use literacy prompts to collect language examples for portfolio assessments. It is the perfect setting to talk about math concepts such as numbers, comparisons, geometric shapes, one-to-one correspondence, and measurements. Think of all the science that just coincidentally appears during mealtimes. Harmonious mealtimes also teach children self-regulation and social skills. Because mealtime is one area that relates to the home lives of most children, it is one of the most likely areas where clear learning can build on prior knowledge. Not all children have books at home. Not all children played with blocks before they came to school. With DLL children, their vocabularies and understanding of different concepts may be unclear because they cannot communicate. Nevertheless, every child knows something about food.

Finally, food is an important component of healthy living, and mealtimes are opportunities to help children learn about good nutrition and the importance of making healthy choices for meals and snacks.

The Classroom Environment

Consider the following ideas for making the classroom environment welcoming for all children:

- ☀ Make or purchase placemats with useful mealtime words and pictures in English and other languages to encourage everyone to practice their new vocabulary in real context. (Visit www.sign2me.com for more information.)

- ☀ Keep serving utensils on hand that are manageable for small children to foster conversation and independence, such as small pitchers, cups that do not tip easily, small serving spoons, and dishes that preschoolers can pass easily.

- ☀ Use a white board to write the menu in English and the other languages of the children in the class, and then point to and talk about the interesting foods, using the words from all the children's home languages.

Language Enhancement Activities

Consider the following ideas for making classroom activities welcoming for all children:

- ☀ Find out the lunch and snack menus in advance so you can learn some key words in the children's languages. Better yet, learn a few relevant sentences or questions in the children's home languages to get mealtime conversations going. Examples: "What's the best food we have today?" "What food is new today?" "What kind of snacks do you have at home?" "This salad is cold. What would happen if we made it warm?" "What do we do if our food is too hot?"

- ☀ Practice conversation starters that relate to your classroom themes. If you are doing a theme about water and who lives in the water, you might want to talk about what fish eat.

- ☀ Make some mealtimes special language times: "See how much all of us can talk in our friend's language today."

- ☀ Make silence work for you at mealtimes: say a comment or ask a question, then be silent to allow plenty of room for your young meal companions to step in and keep the conversation going.

Using Sign Language at Mealtime

What You Need	Key Words	
Posters showing relevant American Sign Language (ASL) signs for mealtimes (purchased or made with the computer)	All done	Please
	Cup	Thank you
	Garbage	Water
Pictures or models of the items to be signed	Juice	Names of relevant foods, such as
	Milk	cookie, cracker,
	More	apple, banana,
Recordings of a few songs about food and mealtimes to provide signing practice	Napkin	bread, or meat
	Plate	

What to Do

- Plan in advance to learn the signs for the key words by finding out what is on the menu for the next few weeks or make notes of what the children typically bring in their lunchboxes.
- Introduce the signs a few at a time, practicing them with the children and showing the photo examples of what the signs mean.
- Get into the habit of using the signs consistently throughout mealtime. Alternate between using them with the spoken word and using signs silently. This highlights the function of sign language for the children and keeps up the interest in learning.
- Help the children understand that signs can help everyone communicate even when they do not speak the same language.
- Show how the signs usually remind us of the word they represent. For example, the ASL sign for cereal looks like the letter C chomping several times as it moves across your mouth and chin. The sign for drink is made by holding the right hand as if holding a glass and putting it up to the lips just like you are drinking.

Extend the Learning

- If the noise level at mealtimes is getting a little too high, give a signal for a "sign language only" period and experience some quiet time where everyone, adults included, focuses on the visual language.
- At other times, add new signs to augment the vocabulary of conversations at mealtimes. This is a great setting to practice sign language because everyone is seated at the same level and it is easy to make eye contact between signers and focus on the communication (Dennis & Aspiri, 2005).

- Be sure to introduce signs that have relevance in other areas of the room and then use them throughout the day. Some signs that are popular at mealtimes and are useful throughout the classroom are: "more," "all finished," "please," "thank you," "yes," "no," "big," and "little."

- Teach the sign for "bathroom" (the closed fist with the thumb sticking up between the index and middle finger—the sign for "t"—is held up near the head and waggled). This is a useful sign for children to communicate their needs without shouting and without struggling to pronounce the words.

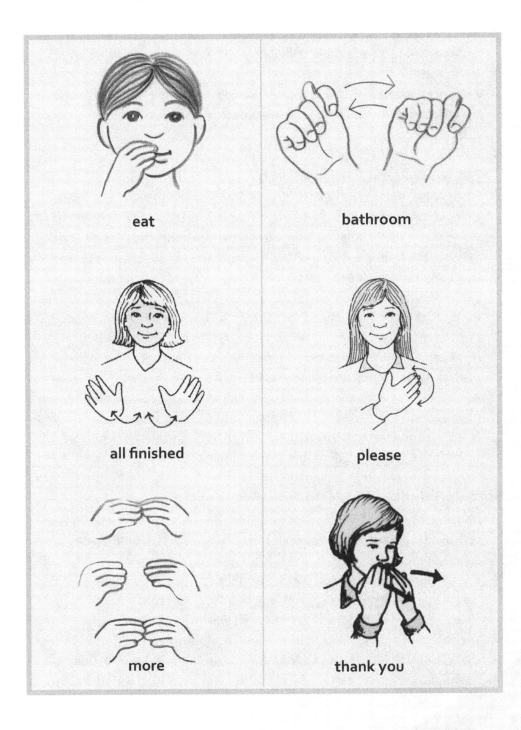

eat

bathroom

all finished

please

more

thank you

Links to Learning Standards

Math

- Count items in other languages.
- Setting the table is one of the best examples of one-to-one correspondence. A child who speaks little English can show her understanding of this by making sure each place setting is complete.
- Sorting by example makes sense at the lunch table for DLL children who may not understand the language.
- Because food is so important to all children, it is easy to capture their attention to demonstrate comparisons: "Whose carrot is the skinniest?" "Whose potato is biggest?"
- Point out the different shapes at the table and use the opportunity to scaffold the children's learning of the English words for the shapes.

Science

- Use mealtimes as realistic opportunities to ask science questions that all the children can understand, such as "How would we eat pudding if we had no spoons?" or "What color would we get if we mix ketchup and mustard?" "How would that taste?" "What tastes good together and what does not?" "Can you tell what this food is just by smelling?" Ask these types of questions in the children's home languages or in English using gestures and real-item demonstrations.
- Revisit themes from the day as they apply to the real experience of mealtimes. "What does this look like before it is cooked?" "What do you think pudding is made of?" Encourage friends who speak the same language to have conversations about these things even if you are not sure what they are saying.
- An important scientific component of mealtime is, of course, nutrition. This is a good opportunity to use various communication methods to emphasize which foods have protein, which vegetables are the best sources of vitamins we need, which foods have sugar, and what foods contain calcium.

Social, Relationship, and Self-Regulation

- Demonstrate how to start and stop while pouring milk. This is good as a table skill, but it is also good practice for self-regulation that DLL children can understand.
- Encourage the children to practice helping their friends at mealtimes by assigning a rotating helper at each table so each child, regardless of language ability, gets a chance to help her friends get what they need.
- The natural use of mealtime to build learning arises because of its free and easy social structure. Robert Stechuk and M. Susan Burns (2005) explain that, "It is often appropriate for teachers to follow the language initiated and used by individual children, who generally use the appropriate language with the people they are speaking with." If you ask a question in Spanish and the child answers in English, that is fine. If she answers in English, that is also fine. And if

the child answers in a mixture of both, that is great too. The point is that the child is motivated to use language in this social setting, and every conversation with a child has the potential to be a brilliant learning opportunity.

Language Arts and Literacy

- Keep a supply of books near the tables so you can look up relevant passages or pictures during table conversations. Then, if a DLL child is asking for something you do not understand, she might be able to show you in the book.
- Ask the children's family members to send in books, recipes, or other information about traditional foods from their countries so the children can talk about them at mealtime.
- Narrate your own actions during mealtime: "Uh-oh, I spilled a little milk. I better get a paper towel to clean it up." Or "This lunch smells good. I think I'll try my chicken first." While the children are sitting and focused, they can really make connections between what you are saying and what you are doing.
- Use explicit vocabulary as you talk about things at the table to make intentional use of every language opportunity for DLL children. Instead of saying, "Please hand me that," say, "Please hand me that metal fork."

Visual and Performing Arts

- Put attractive flowers on the table and talk about them. Why do beautiful decorations make our mealtimes more pleasant?
- Have the children make tablecloths or placemats related to current classroom themes. This is a focus for artistic expression, but it also allows you to reinforce language learning that arises from those themes.

Family Connections

- Ask the children's families to bring in favorite family foods to share, and invite them to sit and converse with the children in their own language.
- With the children, prepare a variety of foods from the children's home cultures, then invite the children's families in to share them. This is sure to spark many interesting interactions.

Classroom Technology Tips

- Use the Internet to research meal-related words in the special dialects of the children in your class. You might also get children's family members to say a few of the chosen words into a recorder or on your voicemail. Because of its homelike and comfortable nature, mealtime can be a prime time to help children practice their indigenous languages or rare dialects. Supporting these declining languages in preschool is so important to prevent such vital aspects of culture from being altogether lost.

- Because mealtime can be a gold mine of preschool conversation, keep a small tape recorder or digital voice recorder nearby to capture examples for portfolio assessment or informal assessment of children's language progress in any and all languages they use.

Questions for Teacher Reflection

Gaining a deep understanding of the multi-layered value of family-style mealtimes for preschool children, particularly DLL children, can be a significant change for school officials and teachers who are accustomed to sending children to a large, chaotic cafeteria for lunch so they can have time to themselves. Teachers and administrators need to work together to take ownership of this important focus in the preschool day and protect developmentally appropriate practice. Personal reflection and shared observations are important parts of this process.

- Does your program's curriculum address mealtime and snack time directly? If so, how do you feel about how well the guidance fits the needs of your DLL children? If not, how might you adapt some of the curricular elements to use during this valuable learning time?
- If your program does not use family-style meals, how can you find another early childhood program that does this successfully so you can arrange to observe the process?
- Ask another teacher to observe your children during mealtime and use her observations as a source of reflection to help you improve these wonderful learning opportunities.

Conclusion

Each child you teach has the potential to become the person who keeps people safe by erecting strong buildings, the doctor who cures an illness, or the parent who raises the next generation of thoughtful, responsible citizens. Children who come to our preschool programs from diverse backgrounds have the potential to contribute to a brighter future for all of us. They present us with new and interesting challenges. This is what keeps great teachers in the field. With so much change, there's no chance for complacency, and many opportunities to make a difference, learn new skills, and help at-risk children succeed.

We know that the first few years in a child's life are critical learning years. DLL children can't put all that learning on hold while they are waiting to fully understand English, and we certainly cannot suspend teaching until the language is mastered. Teachers of linguistically diverse children know they are responsible for facilitating learning for every single child who comes to their classroom. The strategies recommended in this book for supporting DLL children should look very familiar to preschool teachers. These techniques are based on excellent preschool teaching practices to support language and concept learning for all children.

Meeting the needs of growing numbers of DLL children in preschool depends on making great teachers aware that they already have much of the knowledge and skill necessary to connect with DLL children. This kind of self-awareness forms the basis for the kind of intentionality that will enable teachers to differentiate instruction successfully for each of the diverse children in their classrooms.

Above all, we must remember that learning language starts with the child and is controlled by the child. Each child brings his or her own personal style to interactions. It is the connection with other children and adults that moves that language development along. "The motivating force for communication comes from within, from the desire to connect with others and feel the satisfaction that results from that connection." (Weitzman and Greenberg, 2002)

In the next few years, we are likely to see an explosion of research about dual language learners in preschool. The strategies in this book are based on developmentally appropriate practices for preschool. They are designed to be adaptable for a variety of approaches and curriculum models. No matter where the future research leads us, the strategies in this book will be useful for preschool educators.

As questions about updated teaching strategies for DLLs arise faster than research can provide answers, there is bound to be a great deal of trial and error in the classroom. It is crucial that early childhood educators in all areas of the field share what they have learned from their attempts, successful or not, to make high-quality preschool education accessible to children from all language backgrounds.

References

Alda, A. 2006. *Did you say pears?* New York: Tundra Books.

August, D. & Shanahan, T., Eds. 2008. *Developing reading and writing in second-language learners: lessons from the report of the national literacy panel on language-minority children and youth.* New York: Routledge, the Center for Applied Linguistics, and the International Reading Association.

Bodrova, E. & D. Leong. 2007. *Tools of the mind: The Vygotskian approach to early childhood education.* Upper Saddle River, NJ: Pearson.

Chang, F., G. Crawford, D. Early, D. Bryant, C. Howes, M. Burchinal, O. Barbarin, R. Clifford, R. Pianta. 2007. Spanish-speaking children's social and language development in pre-kindergarten classrooms, *Early Education & Development*, vol. 18(2).

Copple, C. & S. Bredekamp, Eds. 2008. Developmentally appropriate practice in early childhood programs, third edition, Washington, D.C.: NAEYC.

Cummins, J. 2008. Bilingual children's mother tongue: Why is it important for education? Internet article: *www.iteachilearn.com.*

Dennis, K. & T. Aspiri. 2005. *Sign to learn: American sign language in the early childhood classroom.* St. Paul, MN: Redleaf Press.

Dickinson, D. & P. Tabors. 2003. Fostering language and literacy in classrooms and homes. In *Spotlight on Young Children and Language*, D. Koralek, ed. Washington, DC: NAEYC.

Dragan, P. B. 2005. *A how-to guide for teaching English language learners in the primary classroom.* Portsmouth, NH: Heinemann.

Espinosa, L. 2007. *Challenging common myths about young English language learners.* New York: Foundation for Child Development.

Freedson-Gonzalez, M. 2008. Presentation at NJTESOL-NJBE Conference, Somerset, NJ.

Genishi, C. 2002. English language learners: Resourceful in the classroom, *Young Children*, July.

Harms, T., Clifford, R. & Cryer, D. 2004. *Early childhood environment rating scale, revised.* New York: Teachers College Press.

Hirsch, E. 1996. *The block book, 3rd ed.* Washington, D.C.: NAEYC.

Jalongo, J.R. 2008. *Learning to listen, listening to learn.* Washington, D.C.: NAEYC.

Lewis, C. 2004. *Lesson study in powerful designs for professional learning*, L.B. Easton, Ed. Oxford, OH: National Staff Development Council.

Meier, D.R. 2004. *The young child's memory for words.* New York: Teachers College Press.

Munsch, R. 2000. *I'll love you forever.* Buffalo, NY: Firefly Books, translation to French by Robert Paquin.

Nixon, M. 2003. The Case for Good Acoustics at Daycare, *Hearing Health* 19:2.

Plutro, M. 2005. Program performance standards: Supporting home language and English acquisition. *Head Start Bulletin #78.*

Rogers, C.L., Lister, J.L., Febo, D.M., Besing, J.M., Abrams, H.B. 2006. Effects of bilingualism, noise, and reverberation on speech perception by listeners with normal hearing. *Applied Psycholinguistics*, vol 27.

Stechuk, R. & Burns, M.S. 2005. Does it matter how adults use children's first language and English when they talk to preschoolers?, *Young Children*, November 2005.

Tabors, P. 2008. *One child, two languages: A guide for early childhood educators of children learning English as a second language (2nd ed.).* Baltimore, MD: Paul H. Brookes.

The Education Trust. 2008. Latino Achievement in America. Website resource guide. www.edtrust.org.

Weitzman, E. & Greenberg, J. 2002. *Learning language and loving it: a guide to promoting children's social, language and literacy development in early childhood settings, 2nd ed.* Toronto: The Hanen Centre.

Index